• Bartholo

WALKING IN
PROVENCE

by Brian Spencer

Bartholomew
An Imprint of HarperCollins*Publishers*

CONTENTS

A Bartholomew Walk Guide
Published by Bartholomew
An Imprint of HarperCollins*Publishers*
77-85 Fulham Palace Road
London W6 8JB

First published 1996
© Bartholomew 1996

Printed in Hong Kong

ISBN 0 7028 3132 8
96/1/15

LOCATION MAP

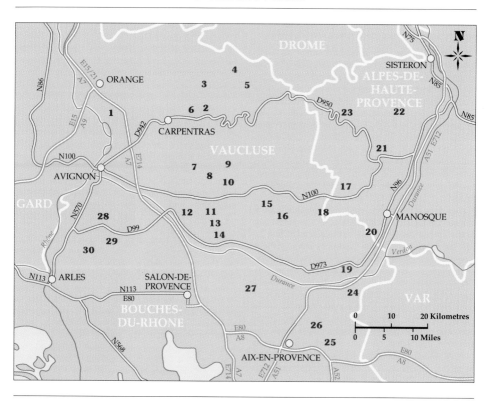

KEY TO ROUTE MAPS

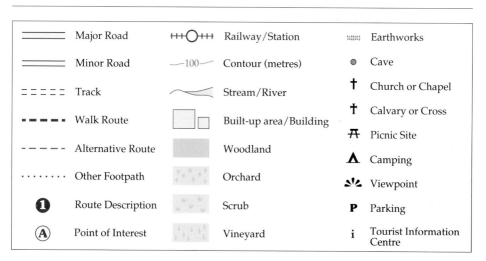

Major Road	Railway/Station	Earthworks
Minor Road	Contour (metres)	Cave
Track	Stream/River	Church or Chapel
Walk Route	Built-up area/Building	Calvary or Cross
Alternative Route	Woodland	Picnic Site
Other Footpath	Orchard	Camping
Route Description	Scrub	Viewpoint
Point of Interest	Vineyard	Parking
		Tourist Information Centre

INTRODUCTION

PROVENÇE – SOMETHING FOR EVERYONE

Everyone has their own idea of Provençe. To some it is the overcrowded coastline of the Côte d'Azur, to others it is a land of rolling forested hills bordering open landscapes of vines and olive groves. It is a land where the brilliant light has attracted artists, from the first Roman settlers to masters like Cézanne and van Gogh. Others come to marvel at the monuments of early civilisations. And there are those who simply wish to find for themselves the true character of Provençe.

While there cannot be any true boundary to a place as complex as this, the region generally accepted as Provençe fills the far south-eastern corner of France. Five *départements*, roughly the equivalent of British counties, cover the region. In the north and to the east of the Rhône, is Vaucluse, including its tiny but jealously guarded enclave within southern Drôme. The rest of the Rhône delta, including the Camargue, is known as the Bouches-du-Rhône. The *département* of Hautes-Alpes fills the north-east corner of Provençe; the remaining mountainous countryside to its south being part of the Alpes de Haute-Provençe. Var and Alpes-Maritimes cover both the Mediterranean coastline as well as the sparsely populated country inland. The eastern part of Gard, while officially part of Languedoc-Rousillon province, considers itself Provençal no matter what officialdom might decree.

The Rhône and the Italian border make the natural western and eastern boundaries of Provençe and the Mediterranean coast marks the southern boundary. While *départemental* boundaries mark the northern limits, there is no natural line where Provençe ends.

THE GEOGRAPHY OF PROVENÇE

As with all types of countryside, it is the rocks beneath the surface that determine the quality of the land. Limestone predominates throughout most of Provençe, creating the rapidly draining soil essential for grape cultivation. Surface water tends to disappear into some of Europe's deepest caves, or finds its way into massive gorges such as the Gorges de Verdon, or the Nesque.

When two massive continents, the forerunners of Africa and Europe, started to collide in prehistoric times, massive pressures from their movement created the Alps and the Pyrenean mountains. Comparatively minor side movements caused ripples which became the rolling lines of ridges that feature in central and northern Provençe. Mont Ventoux, at 1910 metres (6267 feet) the 'Giant of

Provençe', regularly features in the Tour de France cycle race, together with its neighbour the Montagne de Lure, overlook totally different countryside to the south. Chalk, another form of limestone, has created the ideal medium for *Côte de Ventoux* vintages, along with the rich yellow soil exploited by the growers of melons and other high value crops. A little to the east, the arid landscapes of the limestone plateaus beneath Montagne de Lure are more suited to drought tolerating olive trees and aromatic herbs.

The flat alluvial lands bordering the Rhône are some of the richest in France. It is here, in tiny fields sheltered from the Mistral's blast, that early vegetables and soft fruit are grown. Grapes of the Côte de Rhône and Châteauneuf-du-Pape vintages are grown on the sunny slopes above the river. The long dark pine-clad whaleback of the Lubéron ridge forms the central feature of Provençe's only National Park, the *Parc Naturel Régional du Lubéron*. Cut by the River Calavon and with Apt at its centre, the Lubéron is part agricultural, part forest and part a natural wilderness dotted with remote unspoilt villages.

Mont St. Victoire to the east of Aix-en-Provençe towers over countryside which delighted the impressionist painter Paul Cézanne, and is where Pablo Picasso made his home. Bordered by the now tamed Durance river, a high part arid, part forested plateau stretches towards the Alpes Maritime along the Italian border and to their north, the pre-Alps mark the start of the true Alpine France. An area of special geological interest features in the landscape east of the Plateau de Valensol, and has been designated the *Réserve Géologique de Haute Provençe*. Treeless, but filled with rare semi-alpines, this is the route Napolean took following his escape from Elba in 1815.

In the far south mountains abruptly meet the rocky coastline and its offshore Iles d'Hyères. Wide bays around Antibes mark the Riviera, where the turquoise sea of the Côte d'Azur is overlooked from a road carved along the high cliff face. Huge naval depots and commercial ports use sheltered bays at Toulon and Marseille further along the coast to the west.

Inland seas and salt marshes of the Camargue mark the Rhône's joining with the Mediterranean. Only partly tamed, the Camargue is to the west of the delta, while to its east deep man-made channels allow oil tankers to approach refineries alongside a chemical industry based on salt evaporated from sea water.

FLORA AND FAUNA

In a region as complex as Provençe, it comes as no suprise to find that its wildlife ranges from North African to Alpine. Working south from Mont Ventoux, you can find alpine flowers ranging from gentians, cushion saxifrages to drought tolerating moon daisies and purple globularia. Corsican pines and Atlas cedars thrive on the scree slopes below the summit ridges, where the sinister and parasitic yellow broomrape can be found living on the roots of butterbur. Scrub oakland is the favourite hunting ground of truffle collectors. Broom, myrtle and juniper are major shrubs growing amongst tall cedars on the open ridges of lower Provençe. Wild lavender, sage, rosemary and other aromatics grow on the seemingly inhospitable loose stones that pass for soil amongst the rocks.

Meadows spread with farmyard manure bloom with a kaleidescopic array of wild flowers, their variety and colours mirrored in domestic gardens. Exotic shrubs from the tropics thrive happily in public gardens along the coast and inland away from the effects of the seering Mistral wind.

Boars, beavers, roe deer, woodland moths and fire-flies live in the untamed forests. Lizards, butterflies and snakes can be found on the lower open lime-stone ridges, either soaking up the warmth of the southern sun, or searching for nectar in the highly scented flower heads. Frogs of all sizes and colours continue their courtship serenading into late spring, and the rythmic chirruping of hundreds of cicadas rubbing their knees together evokes memories of long hot summer days.

Wildlife more closely associated with Africa lives amongst the white horses and fighting bulls on salt flats and lagoons of the Camargue. Do not be suprised if you see a tortoise, it is a normal resident of the Camargue. The other and perhaps stranger denizen of the wide open waterlands, is the flamingo. Flocks of these exotic birds can be seen dredging the shallow muddy water. The pink colouration of flamingoes comes from the tiny salt water shrimps which make up the bulk of their diet. To see a flight of these beautiful birds against a clear blue sky is an unforgettable experience.

CLIMATE

Provençal climate is closely linked to the dictates of the Mediterranean and seasons change far more abruptly than in northern Europe. With the exception of the highest mountains, where there is often enough snow for several months' skiing, winters are mild, especially along the coast. Late frosts spell disaster for fruit growers and snow on the Côte d'Azur is reported worldwide. The biggest problem in winter is caused by the *Mistral*. This wind is generated by low pressure systems over the Mediterranean sucking cold air down

from the Alps and the Massif Central. As the wind funnels along the Rhône valley it increases in strength, and by the time it reaches Provençe it has become a searching gale. Blowing non-stop for days, and even weeks, it can spell ruination to tender young crops. The wind can cause tempera-tures to drop as much as 10°C (50°F) in a matter of hours and its searching effect is the most hated thing in Provençe. Farmhouses are always built with their backs to the north.

Spring comes quickly and is brief. Summer follows rapidly and with it the searing heat which can even dry up drought tolerating herbs. This is the time when the pace of Provençal life slows down.

Autumn sees the gathering of the year's vintage; a time when an early frost could mean the loss of for-tunes. Once the grapes are off the vines, and with the laborious task of pruning completed, one more circle in the never ending cycle comes to an end.

THE HISTORY OF PROVENÇE

It is almost certain that the earliest humans crossed what was then a land bridge between Africa and Gibraltar, moving steadily along the Mediterranean coast in search of game. Traces of humanoid activity dating from 30,000 BC have been found near Menton on the Côte d'Azur. Later people spread inland, burying their dead beneath crom-lech mounds and erecting *dolmens*, standing stones. At first people lived in circular wood and thatch huts, but needing more permanent homes, they began to build with stone. Based on an elongated beehive design which remained unchanged for centuries, shepherds on the high central plateaux lived in *bories* until this century. Scores of these buildings can be found, especially around Gordes and other parts of the Lubéron.

The partly Celtic Ligurians were the first people to build large settlements and their hilltop strong-holds, or *oppida*, are all that is left of this once flour-ishing civilisation. Examples of their distinctly 'modern' looking art can be seen in museums such as the one at Aix-en-Provence.

Greek traders began to settle along the coast from 1,000BC onwards, founding in 600BC *Massalia*, which became Marseille. Moving inland they settled along the Rhône valley on sites such as the one outside St. Rémy, which later became Roman *Glanum*. The Romans had a hard time subjugating the local tribes, but from 125BC onwards, they spread their control across the whole of Provençe. Using the river valleys for bulk movements, they developed a road system northwards into the rest of Europe.

Provençe became prosperous under Roman rule. Although both Celtic beliefs and the worship of Roman household gods continued in private, Christianity spread rapidly throughout Provençe, and in the fourth century Constantine the Great made it the official religion of the Roman Empire.

Following the breakdown of Roman rule, Provençe came under attack from outsiders who were attracted by its wealth. First came the Visgoths who besieged Arles in AD413, and by AD536 the region was under the control of the Franks. Arabs and Saracens were the next who came looking for spoils, the latter actually gaining a foothold near Hyères along the coast. The Arab advance into Europe was halted by their defeat at the Battle of Poitiers in AD732, but it took until AD972 to finally drive the Saracens out of Provençe.

Anarchy ruled the land for the next three hundred years, until, in 1246, Provençe became part of a kingdom which included Anjou and Sicily. This was the time of the crusades and it also saw the building of a number of great Romanesque churches, such as the one dedicated to St. Trophime at Arles. It was also the time when the courtly art of the troubadours was at its peak. The lyric poets, whose influence spread not only throughout Provençe, but to Spain, Italy and the rest of France, held their most famous Court of Love in the citadel of Les Baux.

French popes, eschewing Rome in 1309, settled in Avignon, and for seventy-seven years the Holy See was administered from a massively fortified papal palace there.

During the mid-sixteenth century whole villages in the Lubéron hills were destroyed. Their inhabitants were members of a fundamentalist Protestant sect known as the Vaudois, who had fled to the fragile safety of the Lubéron from Italy. The Wars of Religion which followed these massacres lasted intermittently from 1560 to 1598.

The eighteenth century saw whole populations wiped out by the plague. This was also a time of great economic instability and political unrest which precipitated the French Revolution. In 1792, a contingent of volunteers marched from Marseille to Paris, and to keep up their spirits during the long march, someone wrote a rousing song which became a hit. Today it is known as the *Marsellaise*, the national anthem of France.

Despite his wide-reaching reforms, Napoleon was unpopular in Provençe. When he escaped from Elban exile in 1815, he can hardly be said to have been made welcome in the region. In fact his life was often in danger and it was not until he reached Gap that he could feel he was among friends. The modern N85 road which roughly follows the route he took, is now known as the 'Route Napoleon'.

The industial revolution, as in the rest of Europe, brought great changes to Provençe. Marshland around the Rhône was drained to create new farmland, canal systems were dug, large span bridges were built and the railway network spread, making it possible to move both goods and people at hitherto unimagined speeds. Ports like Marseille developed and bauxite was mined at Les Baux to make the new wonder metal, aluminium.

Since the horrors of World War II, great changes have overtaken Provençe. Only a fraction of the labour force now works on the land, but agricultural productivity has been vastly increased. Industrial growth is mostly along the Rhône, especially near its mouth where huge petro-chemical plants have sprung up alongside sea-salt based industries. A number of nuclear power and hydro-electricity plants have been built along the Durance valley. But, above all, it is the growth of tourism that has provided the region with its greatest impetus.

FOOD AND WINE

Part of any holiday in France is enjoying its varied cuisine. Every region has its own distinctive flavours and Provençe is no exception.

Naturally enough, fish dishes predominate along the coast. Although *bouillabaisse* is probably the most famous Provençal fish dish, there are others, such as *bourride*, made from grey-mullet, sea bass and other white fish, topped with *aïoli*. *Aigo-sau* is also made from white fish, shrimps and mussels, but is mixed with vegetables, dill and parsley.

Mussels are popular throughout Provençe, as is fish soup, *soupe de poisson*, another dish that has travelled inland. Made from a variety of fish and served with shredded cheese and croutons, it is already quite spicy, so beware the innocent looking sauce served with it. Called *rouille*, or 'rust' from its colour, it is a fiery blend of garlic, chillies and saffron. Eels are also popular; *anguilles sautées Provençales* are shallow-fried strips of eel in oil, together with a touch of garlic and parsley. Salt cod was allegedly introduced by the Vikings who bartered 'stock-fish' in exchange for Provençal wine. *Brandade de morue*, made from crushed dried salt cod in olive oil and milk, has remained a favourite ever since, especially at Christmas. *Aïoli* is a mayonnaise of garlic and olive oil, and is used on a wide variety of dishes.

Tripe may not be everyone's idea of *haute cuisine*, but French tripe does not have the bland image it has in Britain. Try *gras double à la Provençale*, strips of tripe cooked in a stock with bacon, onions, tomatoes, herbs and garlic.

Mutton is especially prized. Served *en brochette*, kebabs of mutton alternating with onion, tomato and green or red peppers are grilled over an open charcoal fire, then served with rice grown in the Camargue. Beef from the Camargue may be served as *boeuf en daube*, a jellied terrine with vegetables, or as *boeuf gardianne*, stewed with herb flavoured red wine.

Although they may now be bred on farms, there are still reasonable numbers of wild boar or *sanglier*. The meat is usually marinaded with herbs before cooking, but can also be served as a roast. Other unusual dishes offered in rural Provençe are likely to be wood-pigeon, rabbit, hare or venison.

The French use a wide range of wild mushrooms, and in autumn whole families can be seen scouring the woods and fields for nature's bounty. Truffle hunting is only for the highly skilled. These astronomically prized fungi are usually found, with the aid of a trained pig or hound, in scrub-oak woodlands in places known only to the hunters.

Cheese comes next on the menu. There is traditionally a cheese for every day of the year in France. Goat, ewe and even mare's, as well as cow's cheese, come in a bewildering array of colours, shapes, pungency and tanginess, and make an important part of any meal.

Locally grown fruits are high on the list of ingredients served in Provençal sweets. Depending on the season, you may find cherries, strawberries, pears, almonds or melons on offfer.

Wines are mostly red, but there are a number of rosés and whites. The best advice is to watch what the locals are drinking, or better still, spend a happy hour or two tasting the vintages at the *dégustations* on offer at the caves of the *négociants*.

FÊTES, FESTIVALS AND MAJOR EVENTS

Almost everywhere down to the tiniest village celebrates its saint's day, when everyone turns out in their Sunday best to walk in procession after the highly decorated effigy of the saint, or the Virgin Mary.

Larger towns host major events, some of international importance, and the following is a selection of events in towns near walks described in this guide. It is worth checking details with local tourist offices.

Aix-en-Provençe
Music, lyrical art and dance festivals; mid-July to mid-August.

Apt
Cavalcade, music festival; Whit Sunday and Monday.
Pilgrimage *(pèlerinage)* of St. Anne: last week in July. Ornamental figure exhibition; November.

Arles
Bullfight festival; Easter weekend.
Fête des Gardians; last Sunday in April.
International festival of music, dance and drama, Roman arena; July.
International photographic exhibition; July.
Festival of the first harvest of rice; September.
Santons (craft) trade fair; mid-December to mid-January.

International exhibition of ornamental figures; January.

Avignon
Horse lovers' event; mid-January.
International drama festival, Palais des Papes; last three weeks in July.
Fireworks display; 14 July.
Jousting on the Rhône; 15 July.
Festival of spiritual games, (tarot, belote etc); All Saints' Day, November.

Les Baux
Midnight mass in St. Vincent's church and pageant of Nativity; 24 December.

Carpentras
Festival of Notre-Dame de Santé; July.
Passion Festival; July and August.
Truffle market; 27 November to 31 March – every Friday.
St. Siffrein Arts and crafts and agricultural trade fair, over 500 years old; 27 November.

Caromb
Festival of Côte du Ventoux Wine; July.

Cavaillon
Comedy festival; April-May.
Ascension Thursday procession; May.
Folklore Fridays; July & August.
Bullfight Saturdays; July & August.
St. Véran Fair, commercial, agricultural and industrial; 4 days around 11 November.

Châteauneuf-du-Pape
Festival of St. Marc; 24 & 25 April.
Lily of the valley *(muguet)*, festival; 1 May.
Fête de la Veraison (marks the time when grapes turn from green to red); 1st weekend in August.
Medieval festival; 1st weekend in August.

Fontaine-de-Vaucluse
Son-et-Lumière; mid-June to mid-September.
Festival de la Sorgue; July.
Music by the Friends of Lubéron; July–August.

Isle-sur-Sorgue
Folklore festival and water procession; end July.
Hunting and fishing exhibition; June.
Provençal market; end July.

Malaucène
Soirées (evening concerts); July.
Summer festival; early August.

Roussillon
International Spring Quartet Festival; June to September.

Sorgues
International festival of jazz; July.

St. Rémy
Organ festival – July to September.

Salon-de-Provence
Classical music and jazz festival; July.
Festival of theatre; July.

Tarascon
Fête de la Tarascon: folklore event; end of June.

Vaison-la-Romaine
Festival of St. John; June.
Folklore festival; early July.
Music festival in Roman theatre; mid-July to mid-August.
Provençal mystery play; first Sunday after 15 August.
Choir concerts – August.
Valréas
Truffle mass in Richerenche; first Sunday after 17 January.
Night of little St. John: 500 year old tradition; 23 June.

HOW TO GET TO PROVENÇE

The road journey from the Channel Ports is long and tedious. The shortest road routes are via the Dover-Calais ferry route, or the Channel Tunnel. From Calais take the A26 Autoroute via Reims to Troyes. The quickest, but not the shortest way south from Troyes is along the A5 to its junction with the A31 north of Dijon. The shorter N71 from Troyes to Dijon could be used, but will be slower. From Dijon the A31 travels more or less due south to link up with the A6 north of Chalon-sur-Saône as far as Lyon. This road continues south to Orange where it divides, the A9 turning south-west to Nîmes, and the A7 south-east as the *Autoroute du Soleil*, into Provençe.

An easier but more expensive way to reach Provençe is to take one of French Railways (SNCF) Motorail Services from Calais to Avignon, Fréjus/St. Raphael or Nice. Trains travel overnight.

TRAVEL IN PROVENÇE

Motor Insurance

Green Card Certificates are no longer required for motoring in France and other member states of the EC. However, you must have an up-to-date Insurance Policy and have advised your insurer about your plans. Your broker or agent will need to know your proposed travel dates and all the countries you intend visiting. Failure to notify your insurer would result in your policy being restricted to the minimum requirements needed to comply with the laws relating to compulsory insurance in any member country of the EC in which the vehicle is being used. Even though travel documents are rarely examined on entry to member countries of the EC, it is advisable to carry your motor insurance certificate and vehicle log book. Your insurance company will advise you about what action to take in the event of an accident.

Holders of UK provisional licences are not allowed to drive in France and the minimum age for drivers is 18.

Motoring organisations also offer extra insurance,

covering personal accident and medical costs, holiday cancellation, loss of personal property, as well as vehicle breakdown, accident and theft. Their insurance schemes cover the cost of replacement vehicles or returning home, either for yourself and passengers, or for the vehicle, should the need arise for it to travel separately. Most foreign travel insurance schemes offered by motoring organisations include Letters of Credit which are repayable on return to the UK.

Driving in France

Motoring in France, despite the need to concentrate on driving on the 'wrong' side of the road, is often more pleasurable than at home. Roads away from the larger towns and outside the main holiday periods are relatively traffic free. However, there are a few simple rules which must be observed when driving in France.

1. Have your motoring documents available at all times.
2. Carry a spare set of bulbs, including indicator bulbs. Failure to do so could result in an on-the-spot fine in the event of any bulb not working.
3. Carry a red warning triangle, and in the event of a breakdown or accident, erect it 30 metres (33 yards) behind your car. It must be in clear view without obstructing oncoming traffic.
4. Wearing seat belts is compulsory for all front seat passengers and drivers. Children below 10 are not allowed to travel in the front seats.
5. 'GB' stickers must be as close as possible to the rear number plate.
6. Drink/driving laws are strictly interpreted and could result in a prison sentence and the confiscation of your car. Random drink/driving checks operate and the best you could expect to get away with, if caught, is a fine in the region of Fr2,000 to Fr30,000.
7. In some built-up areas the *priorité à droite* rule applies and will be signposted. In this case you should give way to vehicles joining your road from the right. However, this rule no longer applies at roundabouts and you must give way to vehicles already on the roundabout, ie those approaching from your left. The sign you will see on approaching the island is *'Vous n'avez pas la priorité*, or *'Cedez la passage'*, which means 'Give Way'.
8. Speed limits (see below), if broken, can earn an on-the-spot fine. Speeding fines are in the region of Fr300 to Fr5,000. Speed limits in built-up areas begin as soon as the name-plate of the town or village is passed, regardless of whether a speed limit sign is shown. *'Rappel'* means 'slow down', and is often prior warning of a lower speed limit, say when approaching a bend or other road hazard.

Speed limits

Autoroutes – (A) roads – 130kph (81mph) in dry

weather; and 110kph (68mph) in wet weather or poor visibility.
National Routes – (N) roads – 110kph (68mph) in dry weather; and 90kph (56mph) in wet weather or poor visiblity.
Other roads – (D) roads – outside built-up areas – 90kph (56mph in dry weather; and 80kph (50mph) in wet weather or poor visibility.
Towns – 50/60kph (31/37mph). The speed in towns varies dependent on road width and other factors.

Parking

Despite what might seem the contrary, there are rules governing parking in French towns. By-laws vary from place to place and, in market towns, from day to day. Parking in some streets is on one side on odd dates, and the other side on even dates. Many places have parking meters (*horadateurs*) but they are usually only for short stay parking; other towns have parking discs which you can obtain at the tourist office. Some car parks have a barrier which opens when a paid-up ticket is fed into a slot.

Preparing the car before driving in France

1. Buy spare bulbs and a spare fan belt, and perhaps a spare accelerator and clutch cables.
2. Make sure the car has been recently serviced.
3. Check the brakes and condition of the tyres – tyre wear rules are similar to those in the UK. Check fluid levels in the brake and clutch reservoirs and make sure the battery acid level covers each cell.
4. Make sure all tyre pressures are correct, including the spare, especially if the car is going to be fully loaded with passengers and luggage.
5. Check the antifreeze content of the car radiator. This is not as strange a tip as it may seem. Antifreeze raises the boiling point of water and will help to prevent boiling, a common cause of vehicle breakdown in hot weather. Check that any hoses have not become soggy and make sure clips do not need replacing.
6. Carry spare fuel in a can (this is legal in France). Have a few useful odds and ends like insulating tape, jump leads, a tow rope and a fire extinguisher. Carry enough tools to make small repairs like tightening cables, nuts and screws, and ensure that the jack will lift the car and the wheel nuts are not too tight.
7. Finally, always carry a first aid kit and learn the basic first aid rules. It could save lives.

To hire a car: toll-free numbers in France
Citer: 05 05 10 11
Avis: 05 05 22 11
Hertz: 05 05 33 11
Euro rent: 05 33 22 11
Eurocar: 05 10 05 05

Useful telephone numbers

An English language update on motorway conditions is available from 'Autoroute Information' by dialling: (00 33) 1 47 05 90 01 from outside France, or 1 47 05 90 01 within France. Traffic information by radio is broadcast on 89.2 or 107.7FM daily.

AA Roadwatch – *UK calls are charged at 39p per minute cheap rate, 49p per minute at other times:*
Continental Roadwatch – 0336 401 904 – traffic conditions to and from ferry ports, major European events and other Continental information.
Motoring abroad; Country by Country – France – 0336 401 869 – laws, paperwork, driving conditions etc.
Continental Roadwatch; French Motorways – Toll Information – 0336 401 884.
European Fuel Prices and Availability – 0336 401 884.
Port Information – 0336 401 891 (Hants/Dorset); 0336 401 890 (Kent).
European Weather Forecasts – France – 0336 401 107.

Health for Travellers

EC rules allow British travellers to enjoy the same health care as French citizens. Before leaving Britain you should obtain Form E111 from the Post Office (this is available to anyone with an NHS registration number). The Department of Health booklet, 'Health Advice for Travellers', explains how to get medical assistance under the French system. The booklet covers what you must pay for and how to reclaim refundable charges, and is available from your doctor's surgery. Chemist shops, *'pharmacies'*, are marked with a green cross and can often deal with minor ailments and injuries, or give advice about where to go for additional help.

What to do in an emergency

For emergency assistance dial 17 for Police, 18 for Fire Brigade, and unless another number is given for Ambulance (usually on a notice at head height, above the telephone in public phone booths), dial 17 and ask for police assistance. Most call-boxes will have emergency and other information in English and other European languages.
In the case of a motoring accident involving a third party, you should inform your insurer's French agent (the address is usually provided by your insurer together with an International Accident Report Form).

Messages about emergencies at home

Persons touring abroad can be informed of serious illness in their family by courtesy of the BBC World Service. In an emergency, RAC Travel Information at Croydon (Tel: 01345 333222) will arrange for a message to be transmitted to the relevant country.

BBC Worldwide Service Broadcasts

The BBC broadcasts in English 24 hours a day.

World news is broadcast on the hour on the following frequencies (in kHz).

Northern France
0500-0730hrs – 6195, 3955, 648
0730-1600hrs – 12095, 9760, 648
1600-2230hrs – 12095, 9410, 6195
Southern France
0500-0730hrs – 9410, 6195, 3955
0730-1600hrs – 15070, 12095, 9760
1600-2230hrs – 12095, 9410, 6195

Telephoning the UK from France

Delete the first zero of the number you are calling. Begin by dialling 19 44, then the rest of the number (minus the first zero); ie to dial a UK number, say (01234) 567890, dial 19 44 1234 567890.

Most call boxes use cards (télécartes) which can be bought at post offices or tobacconist shops. Post Offices are usually open 0800-1900 Monday-Friday and 0800-1200 on Saturday. Away from the larger towns they may close for about an hour at lunchtime.

CONVERSION CHART

1 kilogramme (1000 grams) = 2.2lbs
1 litre = $1^3/_4$ pints
4.5 litres = 1 gallon
1.6 kilometres = 1 mile
1.094 metres = 1 yard
1 hectare = 2 acres (approx)
$20\,°C = 68\,°F\ (\,°C \times 1.8)+32$

WALKING IN PROVENÇE

Walking is almost as popular in France as it is in Britain. Most of the footpath network, especially the well used paths, is kept reasonably clear and waymarked. The Grande Randonnée (GR) long distance footpaths are waymarked by white/red horizontal stripes, and sometimes the route number in black.

Local routes are waymarked with yellow stripes, or other coloured symbols. A waymark turned through right-angles means turn right (or left) at the next junction. If it has a line or cross drawn through it, it means 'do not go this way'; in this case look for another waymark nearby, indicating the correct route. Orange waymarks indicate bridleways or mountain bike (VTT in French) trails.

Provençe has a number of GR long distance routes. The GR4 (Méditerranée – Océan), which links the Bay of Biscay with the Mediterranean, enters Provençe near Vaison-la-Romaine and skirts Mont Ventoux on its way to Grasse by way of Sault, the Gorges de Verdon and Cipières. The GR5 is Europe's longest path, from Holland to Nice; and the GR6 links the Côte d'Azur with the Jura mountains. Finally the GR9, which starts in the Alps, crosses Provençe by way of Sisteron,

Forcalquier, Roussillon, les Baux and Tarascon on its way to the Atlantic Ocean. Several of the walks described in this guide use sections of the GRs, which are highlighted at the appropriate place.

Using this guide

The walks in this guide are comparatively short and are suitable for family groups and individuals of all ages. Most start conveniently from car parks, or near good roadside parking. Mention is made of nearby restaurants or food shops.

Public toilets are few and far between in rural France, but it is normally acceptable to use bar or café facilities, especially if you make a small purchase.

Almost all the walks in this guide use clearly defined paths or quiet by-lanes. If in any doubt , always return to the last recognisably described feature and check again.

The grading of the walks is as follows:
Easy – Fairly straightforward terrain with only slight inclines.
Moderate – As above, but with one or two steady climbs.
Strenuous – Some steep climbs and descents on open hillsides.

Clothing

Boots are not essential for any of these walks, except after prolonged periods of heavy rain, but strong footwear should be worn. Wear lightweight clothing, making sure it will protect your neck and limbs from the sun; also wear a sun hat for the same reason. A light waterproof and a sweater carried in a rucksack guards against an unexpected change in the weather. Also carry a small first aid kit which should contain an insect repellant. A water-based drink is another useful item to carry.

Simple rules for walking in Provençe

1. Walk on the left-hand side of the road and face oncoming traffic.
2. Take your time. Hopefully the weather will be warmer than you are normally used to, and in any case you could miss some interesting scene, or pretty view, by rushing.
3. Before setting out, tell someone about your plans for the day. Some of the walks are in fairly remote areas.
4. Unless they are already open, shut all gates after going through them.
5. Respect growing crops, including hay grass, by keeping to the recognised route.
6. Protect wildlife; do not pick flowers or disturb nesting birds.
7. If it rains, be careful on muddy paths, especially when going downhill.
8. Do not try to make friends with farm dogs; their one purpose in life is to act as guardians!

9. Rabies is endemic in France and domestic animals are usually vaccinated. While the chances of humans contracting the disease are very slim, avoid contact with wild animals, especially if they are acting strangely.

10. Lock car doors and make sure that all windows are closed. As in Britain, theft from unattended cars is a major problem in France.

HOTELS AND CAMPING

Hotels are classified by the French Government 'star ratings', which range from the top 'four-star-L', through three lower grades to the 'one-star' category. Stars are awarded on the basis of the number of bedrooms and facilities, but do not necessarily indicate any recommendation of quality. In fact 'one' and 'two-star' family-run hotels are frequently better places to stay than impersonal high-class establishments.

All hotels are obliged to show their room rates, which are per room and not for each person. Many smaller hotels include breakfast with the room rate. Menus, if the hotel has a restaurant, are also on display either beside the entrance, or next to the reception desk. Unless you have booked in advance, it is normal practice to examine the room before agreeing to take it.

Hotel bookings can be made through the local tourist office, or *Syndicat d'Initiative*, who may make a small charge (see below for addresses).

The *Bienvenue à la Ferme* label, on the silhouette of a butterfly at the entrance to a farm, indicates that it offers rooms and board vetted by the Gîtes de France organisation. Not only will the accommodation and food be to a high standard, but the farm will also have recreational facilities and will be in an attractive setting. Children will be welcome and are often encouraged to help with the animals.

Chambres d'Hôtes (bed and breakfast) are an inexpensive form of accommodation. Frequently in private houses, they are a pleasant way of getting to know the local people.

Many visitors prefer to self-cater and the range of rented accommodation is enormous, ranging from *châteaux* to simple farmhouses, or rural cottages known as *gîtes*.

Camping can be through a pre-booked holiday company, or at one of the well-equipped touring sites in Provence. Many of the sites have shops, swimming pools, hot showers and sports facilities.

Sources of useful information for booking holiday accommodation

Logis de France – a book listing reasonably priced family-run hotels. Available from bookshops, or the French Government Tourist Office (UK address below).

Châteaux Accueil – details of châteaux owners offering accommodation. Available from bookshops or the French Government Tourist Office.

French Country Welcome – 14,000 B&B addresses; available from bookshops or Gîtes de France (UK address below).

Guide Michelin – Red Guide – comprehensive information about towns and places to visit, as well as hotel and restaurant recommendations. Also lists garage telephone numbers. Available from bookshops.

Gault Millau – restaurant guide. Available from bookshops.

LOCAL TOURIST OFFICES

The following are the main tourist offices in or near places mentioned in this guide. Write to 'Office de Tourisme', followed by the place name and address:

Aix-en-Provence
2 Place du General de Gaulle
Tel: 42 26 02 93

Arles
Esplanade des Lices
Tel: 90 96 29 35

Avignon
41 Cours Jean-Jaures
Tel: 90 82 56 29

Almost every small town has its *Syndicat d'Initiative* which will have details of accommodation and events in the area.

FURTHER USEFUL ADDRESSES

French Government Tourist Office
178 Piccadilly
London W1V 0AL. Tel: (0171) 491 7622

Gîtes de France – c/o The French Government Tourist Office, address as above.
Chambres d'Hôtes

Maison des Gîtes de France
35 Rue Godot de Mayroy
75009 Paris. Tel: (1) 47 42 25 43

Logis de France
83 Avenue d'Italie
75013 Paris. Tel: (1) 45 84 70 00

Féderation Français de la Randonnée Pédestre
64 Rue de Gergovie
75014 Paris. Tel: (1) 45 45 31 02

France Information Line – Tel (0891) 244123
Free motorway maps, reference guide etc. *(Calls cost 49p per minute peak rate; 39p per minute off peak.)*

French Railways Ltd (SNCF)
179 Piccadilly
London W1V 0AB. Tel: (0171) 409 3518

Comité Regional de Tourisme Provençe-Alpes-Cote d'Azur
Immeuble CMCI
2 rue Henri Barbuse
13241 MARSEILLE Cedex. Tel: (1) 91 39 38 00

Walk 1
CHÂTEAUNEUF-DU-PAPE

7.25 km (4½ miles)   Moderate

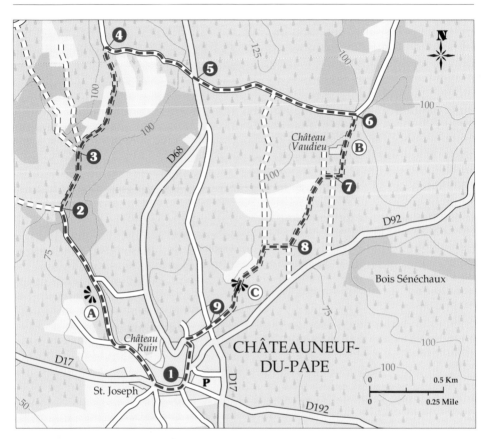

As many as thirteen varieties of grape are blended to make the famous Châteauneuf-du-Pape vintages. 3,000 hectares are filled with row after row of carefully tended vines which climb the hillsides above the ancient town, soaking up the Provençal sun. The soil feeding these vines is mostly chalk, the stark white surface reflecting the sun's rays and so doubling its effect. Châteauneuf is the birthplace of the *Appellation Contrôlée* system, devised by Baron le Roy of Château Fortia sixty-five years ago.

The now ruined château standing proud above the roof-tops and alleyways of the old town was once the 'new' château of the popes of Avignon when that city vied with Rome as the headquarters of the Christian church. Built in medieval times, the hilltop castle was designed to catch the cool breezes rising from the nearby Rhône valley. Its situation made it an ideal summer retreat for the pope and his retinue when the heat, combined with the effects of poor sanitation, made life unbearable in his palace at Avignon.

The walk skirts the foot of the oldest part of the town, then climbs between seried rows of vines to reach a high-rolling plateau to the north. Returning by way of the vineyards of Vaudieu, field paths and narrow lanes wind towards the shade of the town's narrow streets.The old town warrants an hour or so spent exploring its highways and byways.

The ruined château makes an ideal vantage point over the lower valley of the Rhône. There is a museum of old tools and wine presses, the *Musée du Père Anselme*, in the town itself.

Châteauneuf-du-Pape holds two Spring festivals every year, one held on the 24 and 25 of April is to the town's patron saint, St. Marc. The other is on 1 May and honours that loveliest of woodland flowers, the lily of the valley.

As you would expect from a town devoted to the preparation of fine wine, there are numerous caves where you can sample and buy various vintages. There is no shortage of restaurants in the town, catering for every taste.

How to get there: Châteauneuf-du-Pape is on the east side of the Rhône, to the north of Avignon, and stands above the junction of four minor roads, the D68, D92, D192 and D17. Park near the swimming pool *(piscine)* to the east and below the old town.

Route description

1 Follow the D17 for about 200 metres in the direction of Caderousse and turn right uphill along a narrow lane called the Rue des Oliviers. Still uphill, take the lane half right at a junction marked by a wayside shrine, then ahead where the road is signposted right for the château. Begin to go downhill on a steadily roughening track, between extensive vineyards.

2 Ignoring tracks giving access to fields on either side, go half right at a well-used track junction, climbing steadily along a narrow dry and scrub-wooded side valley.

3 Turn right at a complex of four track junctions, then go right again after about 60 metres, uphill along a rough track bordered by scrubland and later by vines.

4 Go to the right when joining the roughly metalled track. Walk on along its reasonably level course, between vines.

5 Cross the road to continue ahead along a minor lane winding through the undulating vineyards.

6 Where the lane descends left to a complex road junction, turn sharp right and downhill along an unsurfaced track, beside a row of trees sheltering red-roofed Château Vaudieu. Still following the track, keep to left of the château.

7 Where the main access track turns sharp left opposite ornamental gates leading into the château gardens, go forwards along the minor track, then bear left between two low flat-topped hillocks.

8 Turn right at an old gatepost marking the boundary of the Vaudieu estate, uphill on a stony track, through vines to a T-junction. Turn left at the junction, then forwards where a short length of surfaced track climbs to a group of farm buildings. Keep on along a narrow grassy track, past scrub oak and other small trees and wild shrubs. Begin to go downhill and bear right when joining the access drive past a group of houses.

9 Go over the minor crossroads, uphill then left and steadily downhill through the lower town in order to reach the car park.

Points of interest

A Viewpoint. Rows of carefully pruned vines following the draining contours of the hillside make a foreground to this wide-angled view of the Rhône valley. Systemic weed killers make sure no other plant can compete with the carefully tended vines, but wayside flowers bloom in profusion away from the effect of the chemical sprays.

B Château Vaudieu is usually open to visitors and you are especially welcome to sample the various wines on sale.

C Viewpoint. Overlooking the hilltop town of Châteauneuf-du-Pape. The imposing ruins of the fourteenth-century castle, which was built as the summer palace of Pope John XXII, have suffered from damage and plunder down the ages, not the least being in 1944 when retreating German forces blew up the keep, preventing its use as an artillery observation post.

Walk 2
SENTIER DE VALLAT

7 km (4¼ miles)   Moderate

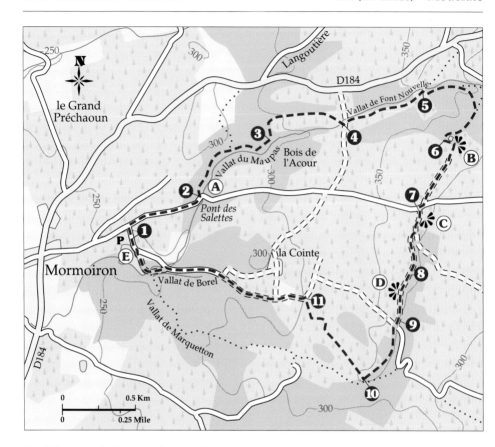

The little town of Mormoiron lies in rolling countryside beneath the foothills of Mont Ventoux. To its west, a rugged escarpment of outcropping chalky limestone gives a hint of the underlying strata of the area. Chalky soil makes an ideal media for viniculture, and it is here that the Mont Ventoux and Roches Blanches vintages are grown.

Mormoiron, like many of its neighbours, was once fortified. Very little is left of its outer wall, but the sturdy hilltop church, dominated by its massive bell-tower, still looks impregnable. The town wall dictated a layout of narrow streets, and many of Mormoiron's houses have outer walls that were once part of the town's defences. One such house, the Portail Vieux, is, as the name suggests, one of the doorways through the town's outer wall. An English couple own the house, from where they run art courses as well as offering holiday accommodation. The address for enquiries is: Portail Vieux, 84570 Vaucluse.

The walk, which can be combined with a visit to Mormoiron, is around vineyards and along an escarpment. It starts by a small man-made lake within easy walking distance of the north-east of the town. Woodland paths follow a narrow valley almost to its head, before wending their way through cherry orchards and vineyards overlooking the nearby village of Villes-sur-Auzon. The tiny tree-shaded reservoir makes an attractive place to picnic.

Mormoiron has a couple of typically rural bars and one excellent restaurant. Prices in the restaurant are very reasonable, but either book in advance or arrive early, as it is a popular venue amongst the local population. They are likely to be drinking the locally produced Roches Blanches wines.

How to get there: Mormoiron sits astride the D14 Bédoin road, about 10km (6 miles) from Carpentras via the D942. Park either in the centre of Mormoiron, or beside the reservoir which marks the start of the walk, about 0.75km (1/2 mile) along an unclassified road to the north-east across the D184, Flassan road.

Route description

❶ Walk uphill from the reservoir in the direction of Mormoiron to reach the minor road. Turn right along the sunken road and follow green/orange and occasional yellow waymarks of the *'Sentier de Vallat'* between vineyards.

❷ Go downhill into woodland by a narrow stream. Do not cross the bridge, but turn left, then right and left again along a woodland path, following green and orange waymarks. Bear right at the next junction, climbing steadily uphill, keeping well to the left of the stream.

❸ High above what has now become a miniature woodland ravine, turn left then right, to walk round a vineyard below a small farmhouse. Follow an unsurfaced access track gently downhill and walk towards the stream flowing through the now shallow upper valley.

❹ Cross the stream and turn left by a large oak tree, away from the access track. Follow a waymarked (green/orange) path between trees sheltering the stream and vines. The path begins to bear left after the first vineyard, to follow the valley bottom.

❺ Leave the stream at a path junction and turn sharp right, uphill, through woodland. Keep to the right at a T-junction, still uphill, then go past the debris of an abandoned stone quarry. Turn left at the next junction and climb out of the trees into fields and make for an old barn.

❻ Bear left away from the barn, following a grassy field track towards an old farm. Turn right to join a sandy access track above another farm on your right. Walk ahead on the sandy, then stony path along the escarpment.

❼ Cross a narrow side road to follow a surfaced woodland track for about 120m (131yds) to where it forks. Do not go downhill on the main track, but continue ahead as indicated by the green/orange waymarks, along the gravel surfaced ridge-top track.

❽ Bear left at a fork in the track continuing along a fairly level course, through scrub woodland, still following the waymarks. Ignore any side turnings into fields to your right.

❾ Go half right then ahead at a four-way track junction, over the crest of a hill, then downhill along a woodland path.

❿ Go to the right beside a ruined barn, following yellow/blue (later blue/yellow) waymarks, steadily downhill and out of the rough woodland lining the crest of the ridge. Begin to bear right as the path becomes indistinct, keeping between the woodland edge and cherry orchards. Eventually a clearer track appears, follow it downhill, moving steadily to your left.

⓫ Turn left on joining a wider (and later to become surfaced) track. Follow it downhill between small vineyards, then ahead at the 45kph sign to reach the lake. Follow the beach to your right in order to reach the car park, or Mormoiron.

Points of interest

Ⓐ The now abandoned old bridge at the side of the road gives a hint of the age of this still rural lane.

Ⓑ Viewpoint. Looking towards the mountainous ramparts of Mont Ventoux - at 1910m (6267ft), the highest point in this part of the Vaucluse Region.

Ⓒ Viewpoint. Villes-sur-Auzon is to the south-east. Surrounded by vineyards and cherry orchards, it nestles snugly beneath the bulky, yet benevolent protection of its ancient church.

Ⓓ Viewpoint. Mormoiron is below, and beyond stretches the fertile ancient floodplain of the Rhône.

Ⓔ The attractive tree-lined reservoir is popular with local anglers and makes an ideal picnic spot. There is even a sandy beach, and swimming is permitted.

Walk 3
LES DEMOISELLES COIFFÉES

6 km (3¾ miles)   Easy

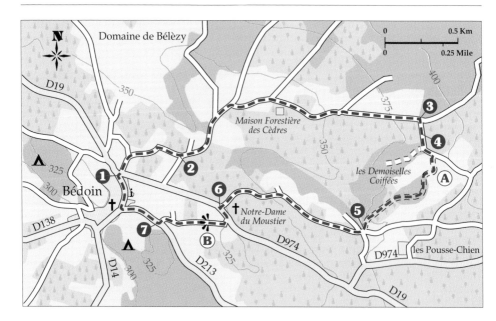

The translation of the intriguing title of this walk refers to young ladies' fashionable hairstyling. The *Demoiselles Coiffées* are in fact a series of rocks. Standing on a low wooded hill, these curious features are the result of uneven weathering of outcrops of softer lower strata protected by a slightly harder upper layer. What is left is a series of tall slender pale sandstone pinnacles capped by darker and harder 'hairpieces'.

The walk begins in the delightful small market town of Bédoin, or Bedouin in the Provençal spelling. Somehow or other Bédoin has managed to stay hidden from the main tourist traffic and is all the better for it. Ochre-coloured houses cluster around a jumble of tiny squares where street-side cafés put temptation into the mind of even the keenest walker. Bédoin's one claim to fame stems from the early days of what was still a new-fangled invention, the motor car. A twisting hilly road to the north of the town is still used for hill climbs. In the early days of this century, no car maker worth his salt could offer a car for sale unless he could boast about its ability to climb the Bédoin hill. Just before the First World War, the record for the climb stood at a little less than 18 minutes. Today's cars take half that time hurtling round the multitude of hairpin bends at speeds of around 145kph (90ph).

About 3km (1¾ miles) out of Bédoin, to the north west along the D19, Malaucène road, the chapel of Ste. Madeleine is one of the most interesting and attractive rural chapels in Provençe. The simple square building is derived from a Roman basilica. Caromb, another village a little further away to the south west along the D138, has an interesting museum based on a collection of old tools.

The walk is ideal for a lazy day. There is little change in altitude, and what little there is makes the going far easier than on absolutely level ground. Narrow, almost traffic-free backroads and field tracks wend their way through vineyards, orchards, lavender fields and plots of high value crops like artichokes. The way is never long out of sight of Bédoin until the turning point of the walk, where a short climb through woodland will bring you to the curious rock formations of the *Demoiselles Coiffées*.

Bédoin makes an ideal base when touring the Vaucluse region of northern Provençe. It offers a wide range of accommodation, from small family-run hotels, bed and breakfast establishments (*chambres d'hôtes*), and four camp sites handy for the town centre. There are a useful number of shops and restaurants to suit all pockets.

How to get there: Bédoin is at the junction of the D974, D213 and D19, about 13km (8 miles) to the north east of Carpentras. The walk starts from the Tourist Information Office at the north end of the town centre. There is usually parking to be found nearby.

Route description

❶ At the junction of the D974 (Mt Ventoux road) and the D19 (Malaucène road), turn right along the D974 and immediately left on a side lane signposted to *Les Demoiselles Coiffées*. Walk past modern houses, bearing right at the next junction, then continue along the lane alongside small vineyards of the Côtes de Ventoux wines.

❷ Go half left at the staggered crossroads, but ignore the private access drive further to your left. Keep right at the next three road junctions, passing the Maison Forestière along the way.

❸ Still following the surfaced lane, turn sharp right at the road junction, moving away from an area of fields and woodland to walk between two vineyards.

❹ Follow the road past an old farm and around a left-hand bend. Ignoring the track to your right on the bend, walk on for about another 80 metres and look for a second track on the right. Follow it into scrub woodland, over a low wooded hill and past the rock formations. Skirting an orchard, walk on steadily downhill through woodland, past another orchard and a small vineyard to reach the crossing of four narrow side lanes.

❺ Turn right at the crossroads, following the narrow surfaced lane slightly uphill, then down past a number of vineyards and two cherry orchards. Later, the lane passes a group of attractive modern houses and old farms before it reaches the main road.

❻ Turn left and follow the road slightly uphill for about 120 metres (131 yards), past the tiny chapel of Notre-Dame du Moustier set back amidst the vines on your left. Look out for a *Gîtes Rural* sign and turn right down a narrow side lane. Follow it hard right as it passes the first house, then on past a vineyard and a scattered group of modern houses to reach the D213 road.

❼ Turn right to follow the road into Bédoin. It joins the town's tree-shaded main street conveniently close to a number of cafés and restaurants. The Tourist Information Office is further along and to the right.

Points of interest

Ⓐ *Les Demoiselles Coiffées*. Pinnacles of soft, easily weathered sandstone have been created by a layer of slightly harder, and therefore more impervious rock. Forming a cap, they sheltered the softer main bulk from further attack by the elements. By chance, these strange obelisks are shaped so that they look, according to local opinion, like young girls wearing elaborate hairstyles. Several pinnacles have rough-cut steps set in them, carved there by budding climbers from the surrounding farms and villages. As the soft rock wears far too readily, and in order to preserve the fragile pinnacles for as long as possible, climbing on them is not recommended.

Ⓑ Viewpoint. Bédoin lies ahead across the seried lines of the *Côtes de Ventoux* vintages. The town curves around the foot of a small, but steep hill. Although no visible trace remains, it was probably once dominated by a fortress. All that is left is the parish church which has watched over the inhabitants of Bédoin for countless generations.

Walk 4
MONT VENTOUX

11.25 km (7 miles)   Strenuous

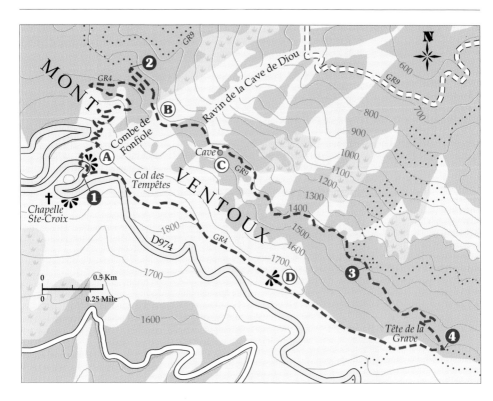

Mont Ventoux is steep and mountainous, and as such must be treated with respect by all who visit it. The walk described here starts on the aptly named Col des Tempêtes, a meeting point of all four winds; in fact Ventoux means 'The Windy One'. The col and its steep access roads are frequently closed by late snows, but in kinder weather a walk along its ridge-top and northern slopes offers some of the widest ranging views in all of Provençe.

The long chalk-backed hump, at 1910 metres (6267 feet) the highest peak in Provençe, was created by massive inward movements when the Alps and Pyrenees were created. Known affectionately as the 'giant of Provençe', the mountain is a frequent stage in the Tour de France, and painted messages exhorting favoured riders can still be seen on the road months after the race has passed by.

The walk, which should only be attempted in fine weather, and then only by those with a clear head for heights, leaves the Col des Tempêtes near the Air Force radar station, then zig-zags steeply down the north side of the ridge beside the Combe de Fonfiole, before swinging to the right across a scree slope on the lower combe. Forest walking on a reasonably level path crosses a series of gullies laid bare by winter avalanches, before climbing up to the open ridge. From here, on the 'rooftop of Provençe', a gently rising path leads back to the col. Choose a clear day for the walk and enjoy the views which range from the Alps to the Mediterranean.

Refreshments are available near the summit of the col, or lower down the road at the Chalet Reynard ski resort.

How to get there: From the south take either the D974 from Carpentras via Bédoin, or the D164 from Sault. The alternative route is from the west by way of the D974 from Malaucène which is on the D938 Vaison-la-Romaine to Carpentras road. All roads are steep and mountainous and should be treated with respect. Park near the Chapelle Ste-Croix more or less at the summit of the pass.

Route description

1 Follow the road northwards from the top of the pass, beyond the radar station and around the first left-hand bend. Take the path to the right of the road, way-marked with the white/red bands of the GR 4 long distance footpath. Zig-zag with care steeply down the bare hillside, steadily moving away from the road, then eventually into the upper limits of the pine forest.

2 Turn right inside the forest, at a path junction signposted GR 9. Follow the contour-hugging path, out of the trees then across an open scree slope and back into the forest. Continue across the north-east slope of the mountain, in and out of forest, and across scree gullies scoured by winter snows.

3 Where the GR 9 path turns steeply downhill to the left, begin to bear right and climb, gently at first, then steeply, zig-zagging through the forest's thinning upper limits.

4 Turn sharp right at a path junction for about 130 metres (142 yards) to join a wider path marked with white/red way-marks and climb beyond the tree-line. Walk up the broad spur of Tête de la Grave, then along the narrow airy ridge leading all the way back towards the Col des Tempêtes.

Points of interest

A Viewpoint. Mont Ventoux has long been a place of pilgrimage for those who appreciate the majesty of mountain scenery. The Chapelle Ste-Croix once gave refuge to travellers along the road, caring for their safety, but nowadays a more sinister note is struck by the radar station guarding French airspace. A plaque nearby commemorates the ascent of Mont Ventoux made by the poet Petrarch and his brother on 9 May 1336.

The views from the col are tremendous. From the viewing table, a vast panorama unfolds, ranging from the glimmer of the sea near Marseille, to the Alps in the north, and on a clear day it is possible to see the 2,800m (9,200ft) high Mont Canigou in the eastern Pyrénées. The best views are either in the early morning or evening when the cooler air brings distant objects into focus. Several alpine peaks of between 3,000 and 4,000 metres (10-13,000 feet) can be seen from here, ranging from the Grandes Rousses (3,486m–11,438ft) in the west, to the Barre des Écrins (4,103m–13,462ft) in the north

B Scree slopes filling the Combe de Fonfiole are regularly scoured by heavy winter snowfalls. Alpine flowers survive in tiny pockets below the protecting bulk of larger rocks, or along the slopes' margins, away from the avalanche zone's worst excesses. Plant life on Mont Ventoux can range from Mediterranean at its feet, to arctic on its bare upper slopes. Woodland trees, such as beech, fill the moist lower valleys, in turn leading to Corsican pines and Atlas Mountain cedars clinging to the sparse, well-drained soils of the middle to upper hillsides.

C A small cave entrance on the right-hand side of the path offers cool and shade on the exposed hillside.

D Viewpoint. Looking back to the south-east along the open ridge. To the far left across the Montagne de Lure are the Basses Alpes and Haute Provençe, then beyond to the Côte d'Azur. A little closer are the high plateaux of St. Christol and Vaucluse, the latter cut deeply by the Gorges de la Nesque. Half right and beyond the Plateau de Vaucluse, the long whale back of the Grand Lubéron marks the centre of a national park which bears its name, the only national park in Provençe. Right again is the Rhône valley, then beyond, shimmering in the white distance, are the still waters of the Camargue.

Walk 5
LE CHALET REYNARD
8.5 km (5¼ miles)   Moderate/Strenuous

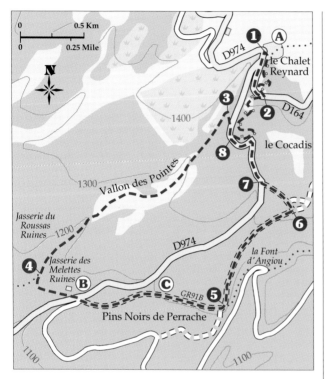

This walk can either be included with an expedition to Mont Ventoux (see Walk 4), or be done as a cooler alternative to the more exposed mountain slopes. The French equivalent of the Forestry Commission have provided roadside picnic sites along roads in the surrounding forest. Interpretive plaques explain much of the history of the forest together with details of its flora and fauna, giving special mention to examples of unusual trees growing nearby. Starting at the small ski resort of Chalet Reynard, the walk soon leaves the open slopes and follows bridleways and forest tracks. The ski lifts behind the chalet are not normally open out of the skiing season.

Chalet Reynard itself is an attractive alpine-style restaurant where you can buy drinks or a full meal.

How to get there: Climb the D974 from Carpentras by way of Bédoin, or D164 from Sault and the Gorges de Nesque. There is ample parking space near the restaurant.

Route description
1 From the Chalet Reynard restaurant, follow the D164, Sault road, downhill for about a quarter of a mile until you reach a number of timber holiday chalets dotted around the forest slopes.

2 Turn right and follow a track downhill between the lower chalets. Cross the D974 road from Bédoin, then bear right, downhill along a bridleway. Follow it under the pines and into a deeply cut dry valley, the Vallon des Pointes.

3 Turn left on reaching the valley bottom, following the track steeply downhill. Go through a clearing and into the forest once again.

4 Turn left at the track junction and climb steadily uphill to the road. Cross the road with care and, ignoring the level forest road to your right, climb the track in front which should be signposted GR 91B and waymarked. Follow it steadily uphill through the forest.

5 Turn left at the second of two adjacent track junctions and climb steeply uphill then across the forested spur.

6 Turn left at a track junction, then left again on joining a more level forester's track.

7 Turn right on reaching the road and walk along its verge until you reach the holiday chalets you passed on the earlier part of the walk.

8 Follow the access track through the chalet complex in order to reach the upper road, where a left turn should be made to reach the restaurant at Chalet Reynard.

Points of interest
A Chalet Reynard, unlike many ski resorts, manages to look attractive in summer as well as in winter.

B The ruins of the Jasserie des Melettes, which once echoed to the voices of a forester's family. Modern transport allows forestry workers to live in the villages around the foot of Mont Ventoux.

C Sun-loving Moroccan and Lebanese cedars thrive on these dry hillsides.

Walk 6
LES ROCHES BLANCHES

6 km (3¾ miles)   Moderate

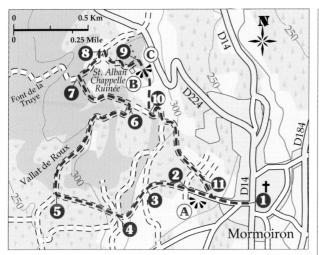

❽ Bear right into the farmyard, then immediately right again and out of it to follow a track uphill through an orchard, then onwards to the ruined chapel on top of the roughly wooded hill to your front. Bear left for about 80 metres, away from the chapel and as far as the survey point.

❾ Turn right to follow a path along the top of the scrub-covered escarpment.

❿ Go to the left at a track junction beside an orchard, steeply downhill, then bear right on easier slopes. Go past scattered olive groves and small vineyards, crossing two track junctions along the way.

⓫ Turn right on reaching the access lane to a group of houses. Walk down it to join the outward lane, turn left and follow the latter back into Mormoiron.

The second walk near Mormoiron takes its title from a long white scrub-covered escarpment of chalky limestone overlooking the village from the west. The title is also the name of the local red and white vintages. The route crosses this escarpment twice with a visit to the romantic ruins of an abandoned hilltop chapel dedicated to the English saint St. Alban. Refreshment can be found in one of the couple of bars in the central part of the main street, or at the attractive family-run restaurant on the northern outskirts of the village.

How to get there: The D942 road from Carpentras via Mazan passes the southern limits of Mormoiron. Turn left on to the D14 Bédoin road. Park in the central square near the post office and Tourist Information Office.

Route description

❶ From the post office turn away from the main street, following a narrow side street for about 100 metres, then turn right climbing steadily uphill out of Mormoiron and past olive groves.

❷ Continue ahead on the sandy track climbing diagonally left towards the limestone escarpment.

❸ Go half left at a track crossing, steeply uphill and over the escarpment.

❹ Cross a complex six-way track junction and continue forwards and downhill through olive groves and scrub woodland.

❺ Turn right on the far side of a large orchard to follow a dry side valley steadily uphill through rough woodland.

❻ Go to the left at the track junction, across the head of the shallow valley.

❼ Turn right at a track junction on the far side of a small vineyard. Go gently uphill to an old farmhouse.

Points of interest

Ⓐ Viewpoint. The Roches Blanches escarpment is a typical feature of the soft banded limestone which occurs throughout this corner of the Vaucluse. Attractive drought tolerating flowers bloom in spaces between the faulted strata.

Ⓑ The chapel is named after the English Saint Alban who was martyred in Roman *Verulamium* (now St. Albans, Herts) in the 3rd Century AD. When soldiers searched his house, and although he was a pagan, he put on a priest's cloak to draw attention away from Christians hiding nearby.

Ⓒ Viewpoint. Looking southeast towards the Plateau de Vaucluse, and beyond towards the rolling hump-backed forested hills of the Lubéron National Park.

Walk 7
FONTAINE-DE-VAUCLUSE

5 km (3 miles) Moderate/Strenuous

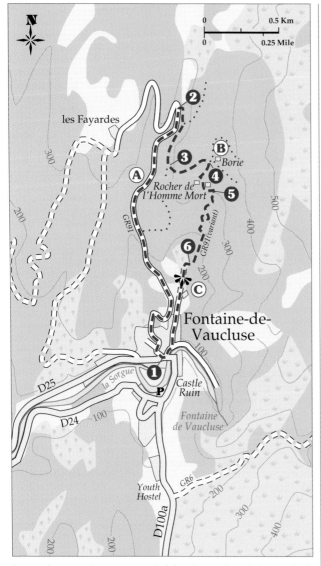

Sorgue, the walk rapidly climbs high above the valley, beyond which stretches the whole of southern Provençe.

The word 'fountain' in the name Fontaine-de-Vaucluse refers to the resurging River Sorgue which appears as a lake at the cave-like foot of a massive semi-circular crag a short distance from the village. On summer evenings *son et lumière* shows are staged by this natural amphitheatre, overlooked by a ruined castle, once the summer residence of the bishops of Cavaillon. For most of the summer and autumn the lake is placid, but in spring, or after a period of heavy rain, it can turn into a violent frothing torrent. Fed by water which has seeped through the porous fissured rock of the district, the river starts far beneath Mont Ventoux and the Lubéron heights. A local speleologist, Norbert Casteret, spent 30 years tracing the underground course of the emerald green waters of the Sorgue. A museum devoted to his lifetime's work is in Fontaine-de-Vaucluse.

An aqueduct built in Roman times carried the waters of the Sorgue as far as Arles. Part of that structure can still be seen at the roadside of the D24, near the village of Galas.

Fontaine-de-Vaucluse has been inhabited since at least Roman times. A still functioning Gallo-Romaine fountain head can be seen in the lower town. The Italian poet Petrarch retired here from Avignon between 1327 and 1353. A

Strong footwear is recommended for this walk. While the climb out is comparatively easy and straightforward, the return is downhill and along a steep rocky woodland path, and can be difficult, especially after prolonged rain. Nevertheless, the walk has its attractions. Starting beside the exuberant infant River

column in the main square honours his links with Fontaine. He wrote a great number of his poems while living in Fontaine, many of which speak of his unrequited love for Laura of Avignon, and his fondness for the solitude of Fontaine-de-Vaucluse, which he called his *Vallis Clausa*, the Closed Valley. A small Petrarch Museum is on the site of what was thought to be his house. Other museums in the town are devoted to local crafts, the history of rationing in France during the last three European wars, and of all things in such a tranquil place, the history of punishment. The latter houses several rather gruesome exhibits.

Water power from the River Sorgue drove paper mills along the valley. Most are closed and abandoned, but examples of high quality locally manufactured note-paper can be bought nearby.

To cater for its popularity as a tourist centre, Fontaine-de-Vaucluse has a comprehensive range of places to eat. Most are along the riverside and offer an attractive end to a walk across the nearby heights.

How to get there: Fontaine-de-Vaucluse is at the junction of the D24 and D25, about halfway between Gordes and l'Isle-sur-la-Sorgue. Although there is a town centre car park,

it is advisable to park by the riverside on the outskirts rather than attempt to drive along the narrow central streets.

Route description

❶ From the river bridge walk to the left of the *Mairie* and past the Gallo-Romaine fountain. Follow the winding streets uphill and to the right of the tennis courts and into the upper car park. Go through the car park, still uphill and out along a narrow lane. Follow the lane towards the wooded slopes cut by bands of overhanging limestone crags. Follow white/red waymarks of the GR 91 long distance footpath, uphill for 2 km (1¼ miles).

❷ Where the road makes a sharp left-hand hairpin turn, turn hard right and away from the road and join a woodland path. Ignore a wider track to the left and climb gently beneath the trees, following waymarks of the GR 91 Variant.

❸ Turn left and climb a little more steeply uphill at the path junction.

❹ In sight of a ruined building and at a cross tracks, turn right and begin to go downhill to a group of more ruined buildings. Bear left towards the top of a limestone cliff marking the start of a steep wooded combe.

❺ Take great care and follow the zig-zagging course of the path, steeply downhill through the trees.

❻ Reaching open fields and a small orchard, bear a little to

your right, then left, and descend to reach a small farm. Follow the narrow, but steadily improving access lane downhill into Fontaine-de-Vaucluse, entering the town conveniently near the riverside restaurants.

Points of interest

Ⓐ The lane uses a natural break along a line of weakness in the soft oolitic limestone to reach farms on the easier upper slopes. The word *oolite* comes from the ancient Greek word for fish roe, an apt description for this finely grained yet soft stone.

A prominent rock on the far side of the narrow valley is called the *Rocher de l'Homme Mort*, the Cliff of the Dead Man. Below it, and even more curiously named, are the *Roches Baumes*, the Balm or Calming Rocks.

Ⓑ The ruined building (and others lower down the slope) is an example of a *borie*, an ancient hovel where the roof stones are cantilevered one on top of another without the aid of timbers, creating an elongated beehive effect. These dwellings were probably once used by shepherds on the annual migration to higher pasturage, or by woodsmen cutting timber to be made into pulp, the first stage in paper making.

Ⓒ Viewpoint. Pause for breath and enjoy the view of the village and its ancient mills fitting snugly between two bends of the river. The Sorgue's birthplace at the foot of a natural amphitheatre can be seen a little to the left of the village.

Walk 8
GORDES AND ITS *BORIES*   7.25 km (4½ miles)   Moderate

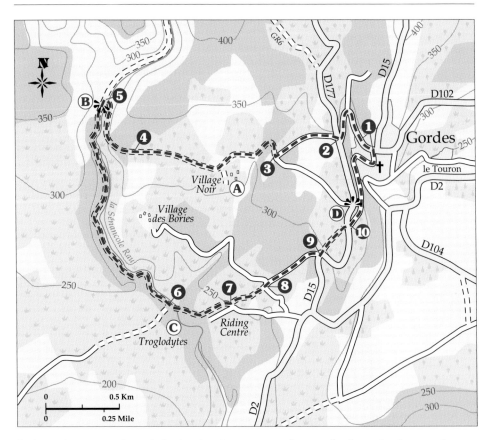

Bories, ancient stone, often windowless hovels, are scattered across the dry rocky slopes to the west of Gordes. Numbers of them, in various states of repair, are seen on this walk. Roofed with small cantilevered overlapping stones, *bories* were the homes of peasant farmers and shepherds not so very long ago. Those still in any state of preservation around nearby farms are used as barns. A restored *borie* village lies to the north-west of pointer ❸ on this walk; it can be visited either as an extension of the walk, or by car later.

Gordes, where the walk starts, is still heavily fortified. It sits on top of a high crag overlooking mellow-stoned, pantile-roofed ancient houses built on narrow terraces above vineyards and olive groves of the dry surrounding countryside.

Important in medieval times, Gordes gradually sank into decline as more modern events overtook it, but in the 1920s it began to recover when it was 'discovered' by the artist André Lhote. The town suffered a setback in 1944 and was severely damaged following the Allied invasion of southern France. Gradually normality returned, and with it came artists who have made Gordes their home. The château houses the Vasarely Museum, devoted to the modernistic works of the Hungarian born artist. Nearby, and reached by a complex system of roads culminating in the D148, is a museum devoted to the work of the stained glass artist Frédérique Duran.

Not far away from Gordes, to the north-west along the D177, the monks of Sénanque Abbey make a strongly flavoured herb-based liqueur called Sénancole, developed, as most liqueurs were, from a secret formula. The abbey was founded in the twelfth century by Cistercian monks who were driven out during the Revolution. Abandoned, and in decay for two hundred years, the abbey is steadily being restored. Inside the abbey a museum devoted to the Tuareg people traces the lifestyle of the 'blue men of the Sahara'.

The walk follows the D15 away from Gordes then crosses a dry, rocky, scrub-covered sloping plateau to the west, before dropping steeply into the dry valley of the Sénancole. A gradual climb leads back to the D15 and the rewarding view of Gordes.

There are several moderately priced restaurants around the town square in Gordes, and also food shops.

How to get there: From Cavaillon take the D2 north-east to Gordes, or the D4 and D2 north-west from Apt. Park in one of the signposted car parks a short distance from the town centre.

Route description

1 Walk away from the castle and the town square, following the D15 downhill and round the tight bend as far as its junction with the D177.

2 Turn right on to the D177 (Sénanque Abbey road), and almost immediately go left along a narrow walled lane.

3 Go to the right at the T-junction, following the rough track across a shallow side valley, through scrub woodland and past olive groves and the access drives to small farms.

4 Beyond the last farm, and approaching rough woodland, the track narrows and begins to descend to the right into a dry valley.

5 Keep to the left at the track junction in the valley bottom, following it into increasingly dense rough woodland.

6 Turn left at a cross tracks and climb out of the Sénancole valley, first going uphill in scrub, then on an improving surface past an olive grove.

7 At the track and lane junction opposite the riding school, turn left on to a rough woodland track.

8 Join a narrow high-walled lane; (it gives access about 1.25km – ¾ mile – on your left, to the restored *borie* village). Follow it ahead and over the next T-junction, past the entrances of several small farms and attractive houses where old *bories* are now garden features.

9 When the side lane reaches the main road, turn immediately away from the road to follow a trackway between a series of olive groves.

10 Cross the main road and go steeply down the side road opposite, across the dry valley to climb by side alleys into Gordes.

Points of interest

A A side track on your left leads through the scrub to an abandoned *borie* village.

B Viewpoint. Looking down the dry valley bed of the Sénancole. Brightly coloured semi-alpine flowers grow on the dry limestone soils.

C About 150 metres downstream of pointer **6**, cave-like dwellings cut into the outcropping limestone were used well into this century.

D Viewpoint. A short but worthwhile diversion, about 100 metres to the left along the road from pointer **10**, leads to a spectacular natural viewing platform overlooking Gordes.

Walk 9
MURS

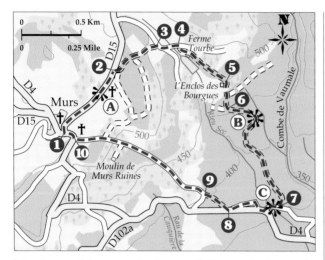

Murs is one of those completely unspoilt Provençal villages. The meaning of its name is somewhat vague. Certainly 'murs' in modern French means 'walls', but if that is so, then where are the walls? The village fits snugly to the top of a small rise, but in no way does it appear to have ever had a defending wall built around what is still its outer boundary.

The walk starts near the old château, and follows trackways and quiet roads around lavender fields and ancient woodlands.

Murs has one small family-run restaurant.

How to get there: Murs stands above the junction of the D4, Apt to Carpentras road, and the D15/D5 road between Gordes and Sault. The village proper is closed to all except local traffic, but safe roadside parking may usually be found near the turning towards the church and château.

Route description

❶ Follow the D15 north-east in the direction of Sault.

❷ Turn right at the wayside shrine set back to the right away from the road. Go immediately to your left on a rough track, through woodland and to the right-hand side of lavender fields. Ignore a side turning on your right after about 250 metres, then begin to swing gently to the right as you walk downhill.

❸ Turn right to follow a narrow surfaced lane, across a dry valley and past a fish pond.

❹ Turn right beyond the pond, along an unsurfaced track. Keep to the left of Tourbe Farm (Ferme Tourbe), following the right of way.

❺ Skirt the old farmstead of l'Enclos des Bourgues by following the track to the right around the buildings. Go forward into woodland, then take the right fork after 100 metres.

❻ Go hard left at the T-junction with a minor woodland track, and go downhill on a gradually steepening slope, keeping roughly equidistant between two valleys, the one deep-cut to your left and the other slightly wider, but shallower.

❼ Turn right where the track joins an abandoned stretch of road. Cross the old bridge and climb up to the modern road, then turn right. Follow the road for about 80 metres to go right again along a further stretch of the old road.

❽ Where the old road rejoins the new, do not follow it, but turn right on to a woodland track, climbing gently uphill past scented shrubs such as rosemary, juniper and wild lavender.

❾ Turn right where you join a minor road, following it steadily uphill past orchards, vineyards and olive groves.

❿ Go ahead past the tiny wayside shrine to join the main road yet again, and follow it for the short way into Murs.

Points of interest

Ⓐ Viewpoint. Look back along the road to the attractively haphazard grouping of houses that go to make up Murs. Above the sagging pantiled rooftops, a square-cut church tower has watched over the area's fortunes and misfortunes down the centuries. To the left of the village, and on a little wooded rise where it would catch the wind, there once stood the local windmill where the villagers ground their corn in days gone by. Sadly, modern methods have superceded this 'free energy' system.

Ⓑ Viewpoint. Two stream beds flow almost parallel to each other. The stream to your right only flows in spring or after prolonged rain, but the other, to your left, is deeper cut and has a stream along its shady depths for most of the year.

Ⓒ Viewpoint. Looking from the bridge into the leafy depths of the Rieu Sec (Dry River in Provençal). Its rare waters flow south to join the Calavon, Lubéron's main river.

26

Walk 10
ROUSSILLON AND THE VAL DES FÉES   4 km (2½ miles)   Easy

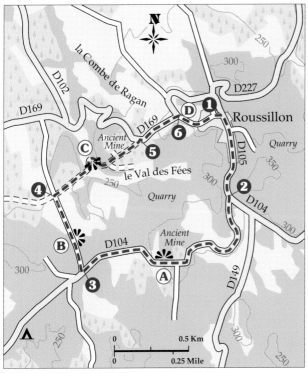

Route description

❶ Follow the ridge-top road south and away from the centre of Roussillon, in the direction of Apt.

❷ Fork right on to the D104 Goult road for 1.5km (a little under a mile).

❸ Turn right and go downhill along a woodland side road.

❹ Turn right at the crossroads and go uphill, then down, on what becomes a gravel track. Cross a wide green valley, between woodlands and small properties. Bear right to climb the other side of the valley, then left at a track junction and ahead at the next.

❺ Go to the right on joining the road, climbing it uphill beneath the shade of mature trees, towards the village.

❻ There are several ways into the upper village; try and ignore roads open to traffic and follow the old alleyways and lanes.

Points of interest

Ⓐ Viewpoint. Looking across the Val des Fées towards Roussillon.

Ⓑ Viewpoint. Spend time wandering amongst the curiously shaped and many hued rock formations of 'The Fairies' Needles'.

Ⓒ Viewpoint of the lower section of the Val des Fées.

Ⓓ Notice how the soft, easily worked rock has been cut away to make a garage.

Weirdly-shaped ochrous rock formations surround this ancient town. Once mined for their colours, the local soft sandstone rocks vary in shades from cream to intensely red-brown hues. An outcropping group of rocks in woodland to the west and below the village have been worn into all manner of shapes, giving them the title 'The Fairies' Needles'. The quarries of Roussillon have been abandoned for some time, but those around nearby Gargas still produce a wide range of colours, including grey, pink and green.

The short walk is mostly on quiet roads and tracks giving ample time to explore the side ravines and rock formations below the town. A fairy glen completes the gentle tour of this strange yet attractive area.

Roussillon is a popular place to visit and so has many shops and restaurants.

How to get there: The D104, D108, D199 and D227 all link with the D4 north-west of Apt via the N100. Follow signs through Roussillon to reach the car parks.

Walk 11
OPPÈDE-LE-VIEUX

6 km (3¾ miles)   Easy/Moderate

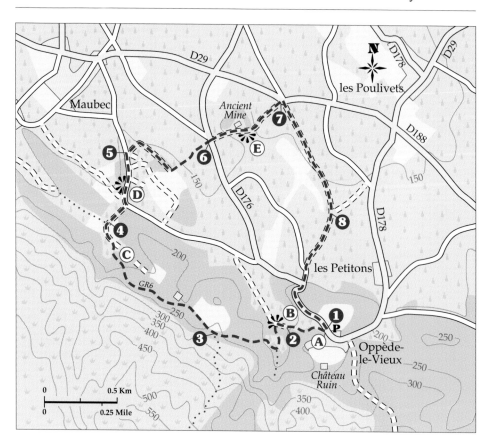

The ruins of a long-abandoned medieval château fill the site of an even more ancient fortress, where stone age settlers held their enemies at bay. The present day village of Oppède-le-Vieux clusters romantically around the mellow ramparts of its old château, high on a rocky hilltop.

Built to command the view over the surrounding countryside in less peaceful times, the village now looks out on to a tranquil scene of vineyards and slumbering farmland along the Cavalon valley.

From Oppède-le-Vieux, the walk follows ancient woodland pathways through dramatic rock scenery in the foothills of the Petit Lubéron heights. You then reach the gentler terrain of rolling vineyards. Skirting the nearby village of Maubec, field paths, farm tracks and back lanes lead back in a wide sweep to Oppède.

It is possible, but not at all certain, that you may encounter wild boar (*sanglier*) on this or any of the other woodland walks in the Lubéron. Do not be afraid of them, but on no account try to attract their attention. The best plan is to stand still and remain silent and they will certainly move away. Only in the remote chance that they become aggressive should you shout or wave sticks at them.

There is a highly recommended restaurant next to the car park at the start of the walk, or others in nearby Ménerbes.

How to get there: Oppède-le-Vieux lies at the foot of the Petit Lubéron, about eighteen kilometres (11 miles) as the crow flies south west of Apt. The quickest way to reach it by road is to take the N100/D2 (Cavaillon road) west from Apt as far as Beaumettes, then turn left on to the D29 to a crossroads south of les Poulivets, and onwards along the D178 to Oppède.

A much more attractive alternative, especially for anyone who has read and enjoyed Peter Mayle's *A Year in Provence,* will be to drive south west from Apt on the D3 to Bonnieux. From there follow the D109 to Lacoste, then on to Oppède-le-Vieux by way of Ménerbes.

There is a small official car park beneath the old village ramparts.

Route description

1 Turn left out of the car park and walk to where the road swings right. Go forwards and downhill on a narrow footpath as indicated by an arrow, between the woodland edge and an orchard.

2 Go past the farmhouse of Tombereau and follow its access drive for about 80 metres and turn left, following white/red waymarks of the GR 6, slightly uphill and through a small vineyard. Bear right at the next path junction as indicated by the waymarks, uphill into woodland.

3 Ignore the path climbing steeply to your left and continue ahead, downhill. Bear left as you approach a lone house, uphill towards, then along the base of the high limestone cliffs. Bear right then begin to go downhill into a vineyard. Join a farm drive and follow it.

4 Leaving the white/red waymarks, turn right along a farm lane to reach a by-road. Go to the left and follow the road for about 350 metres, between scrub oak woodland, and past a vineyard and three access turnings.

5 Look out for a small electricity transformer station on the right, marking the turn along the woodland Chemin de Sarrette. Follow the lane between scattered modern properties then bear right beyond the last house. When the track reaches a number of vineyards, go to the left along the grassy path as dictated by the field boundaries. If the way has become overgrown, aim towards the group of buildings opposite, below and to the right of a low wooded hill.

6 Cross the road and follow the surfaced lane opposite, past a large farmhouse and to the right of the low wooded hill. Go forwards and downhill on a gravel track where the surfaced lane turns left.

7 Reaching the main road, turn immediately right and away from it, along a field track pointing towards the forested high limestone crags.

8 Swing right as you reach a wider track, through vineyards and past orchards, uphill to join a minor road. Turn left along this and, on reaching the village access road, turn left again to climb back to Oppède.

Points of interest

A Visit the hilltop ruins before starting the walk. Tiny ancient cobbled alleyways and stony tracks lead towards the highest point, past pretty cottages. The view north across the valley of the River Calavon takes in most of central Lubéron and beyond to the heights of the Vaucluse.

B Viewpoint. A windpump on the far side of the vineyard must lift water from a great depth in this arid limestone region.

C White and red waymarks indicate the route of the GR 6, the long distance walking route known also by its title *Alpes-Océan,* between the Alps and the Atlantic Ocean.

D Viewpoint. The scattered village opposite is Maubec. It had a castle in medieval times, but little of it remains.

E Viewpoint. White limestone cliffs, partly masked by dense woodland, make an attractive backdrop to the ancient settlement of Oppède-le-Vieux, rising above its vineyards and orchards. To the left, and across the rolling farmland, the houses of Ménerbes seem to cling like limpets to the whale-backed hillside.

Walk 12
ROCHERS DE BAUDE

6.25 km (4 miles)   Strenuous

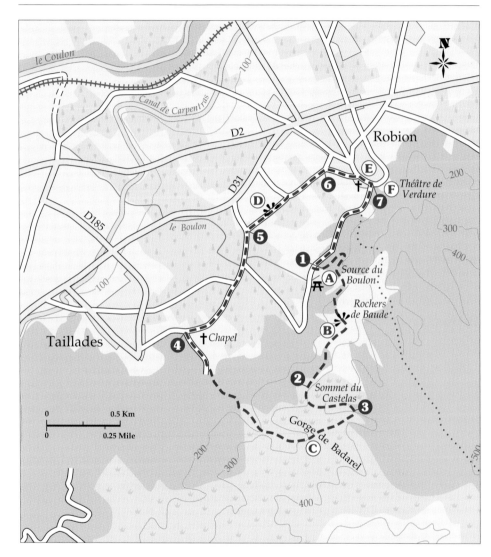

The long whaleback of interconnecting summits forming the Petit and Grand Lubéron, the central massif of the Lubéron National Park, end abruptly in the west. High limestone crags overlook the plains surrounding Cavaillon and the River Rhône.

This walk follows a path that climbs along carefully engineered ledges and steeply works its way through the outcrop known as the *Rochers de Baude* to the south of the village of Robion. Winding its way beyond the crags, the path skirts their upper limits, through forest and across the heads of dry gullies, before returning to lower ground near Robion's neighbouring village, Taillades. Strong footwear is essential and the walk is unsuitable in wet weather. As one or two rocky ledges are exposed, the walk is not recommended for anyone who does not have a good head for heights. Special care must be taken when descending into the Gorge de Badarel at route pointer ❸.

Robion only has a small old-fashioned bar, but it does have a good charcuterie and boulangerie where you can buy the essentials for a picnic. As the walk is steep in its early stages, it is advisable to carry a drink, especially on a hot day.

How to get there: Robion is to the south of the D2, Cavaillon to Gordes road, about 6 kilometres (3¾ miles) east of Cavaillon. If approaching from the direction of Apt, follow the N100 to Coustellet and turn left on to the D2.

Drive towards the open-air theatre in Robion and turn right in front of it to follow the narrow one-way road signposted to Boulon, mostly downhill, past an old quarry. Park on the left beside the stream next to the picnic site at the *Source du Boulon*.

Route description

❶ Walk towards the crags above the picnic site and look out for a rocky path on the left of the stream where it issues from a small cave. Follow this path uphill and begin to swing right through scrub woodland, winding your way towards the upper crags. Do not deviate, but follow the twists and turns of the path, climbing ever higher in and out of woodland and along rocky ledges. Ignore any minor side turnings or short cuts.

❷ The path turns left for its last, but steep climb to the rocky outcrop of the Sommet du Castelas.

❸ After a short reasonably level stretch, the path swings right and descends steeply into rocky confines of the Gorge de Badarel. Follow the rocky path through the gorge. On reaching more level ground, leave the woodland and join a farm lane going gently downhill past small vineyards and tiny fields.

❹ Where the farm lane joins a wider road coming from nearby Taillades, turn right and follow the vineyard-lined road, past a small chapel and scattered groups of farms and houses. Ignore side lanes and continue ahead on joining a second and wider road from Taillades. Go over a small stream, the Boulon, and climb towards the group of houses built around a wooded spur interspersed by vineyards and small orchards.

❺ Where the road swings left around the low hillside, turn right along the Rue de Roumanière, uphill then down, past several modern houses.

❻ Bear right along narrowing backstreets, past interesting old houses and into the centre of Robion. Walk to your right through the main square, then uphill and to the left of the church, towards the open-air theatre.

❼ Turn right in front of the open-air theatre, the *Théâtre de Verdure,* then bear left at junctions, climbing out of the village past scattered properties and into woodland. Follow the narrow lane over the rise past the old quarry, then downhill to reach the picnic site and car park at the Source du Boulon.

Points of interest

Ⓐ After its subterranean wanderings beneath the limestone strata of the Petit Lubéron, the Boulon happily emerges into daylight through a 'letter-box' opening at the foot of the limestone crag. From here it flows in a north-westerly direction towards Cavaillon to join the Coulon, itself a tributary of the nearby Rhône.

Ⓑ Viewpoint. Pause here to catch your breath as the climb is far from over. The view to the north is a patch-work quilt of orchards and vineyards surrounding the town of Isle-sur-la-Sorgue, where its namesake river is split into five branches, each of which once drove a water mill.

The mills are long gone, but a restored waterwheel still turns in the public gardens.

To your left, and closer to hand, is Cavaillon. The ancient town dates from Roman times and sits at the foot of the Colline St. Jacques mountain. Despite only being a mere 180 metres (590 feet) or so at its highest point (and lower than your vantage point) the hill looks almost alpine from this angle. Cavaillon is the commercial centre for the fruit-growing area and has an interesting thirteenth-century cathedral built in the Provençal style. Finds from the town's past include Greek as well as Roman remains and a reconstructed Roman arch; these are on display in the local museum.

Ⓒ The Gorge de Badarel was created by melt-water exploiting a weakness created by a fault in the limestone rocks, creating a wilderness of boulders and small crags where semi-alpine flowers grow.

Ⓓ Viewpoint looking across the vineyards and orchards of the Coulon valley. Closer to hand are the overgrown remains of ancient terraced field systems.

Ⓔ On your left as you enter the square, the Café de la Poste is a small bar-cum-betting shop, a place full of character, and characters!

Ⓕ The Théâtre de Verdure, an open-air theatre, is built into an abandoned quarry. Making use of the natural acoustics, concerts and shows are staged throughout the summer months.

Walk 13
LE FONT DE L'ORME
4 km (2½ miles)   Easy

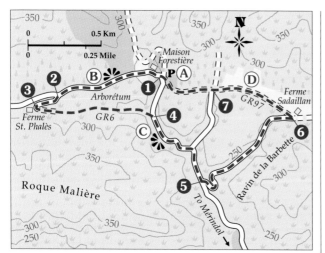

The road leading to the start of this walk is the rough lane servicing a Maison Forestière at the head of a dramatic limestone gorge, the Ravin de Sabatier. Starting from an arboretum collection of endangered shrubs and fruit trees, this forest and limestone valley walk is on easy-to-follow lanes and trackways.

This is a lovely area to explore on a hot sunny day. Every turning has something to delight the eye. Butterflies and rare birds flit among the flowering shrubs and wild flowers, safe from the effects of modern farming methods.

The nearest place to find refreshment is in Mérindol near the start of the access road.

How to get there: The Maison Forestière road is signposted from the north side of the D973 Pertuis/Cavaillon road, to the west of Mérindol. Follow the narrow valley, past a plaque giving details of the road's rebuilding after disastrous floods many years ago, to the road end. Park at the picnic site next to the arboretum.

Route description
❶ From the arboretum car park, turn left to follow the unsurfaced private road, uphill through woodland. Go between two tall stone gateposts and past a large vineyard on your right and an olive grove to the left, heading towards the rooftops of St. Phalès farmstead showing above the surrounding trees.

❷ Turn left and go down the drive towards the farm.

❸ Look for the white/red waymarks of the GR 6 long distance footpath and turn sharp left just before you reach the farm, along a forest track winding its way across, then down the densely wooded hillside. The track narrows to a path soon after leaving the farm.

❹ Turn right on joining the rough road in the valley bottom. Follow it as far as the second junction with side roads.

❺ Turn left and uphill on to the narrow side road, following it above the tree-shrouded Ravin de la Barbette.

❻ Go to the left to follow a woodland track below the farm buildings of Sadaillan Farm, following white/red waymarks of the GR 97, along the forest edge and to the left of a series of vineyards and olive groves.

❼ Continue forwards at the cross tracks, past more vineyards to reach the Maison Forestière. Walk through the arboretum to reach the car park.

Points of interest
Ⓐ The newly-planted arboretum nearest the car park is a collection of endangered species of fruit trees and ancient varieties from the nearby Petit Lubéron forest. Interpretive plaques explain (in French) the trees growing in the arboretum and details of work carried out in the Petit Lubéron Forest. Traditional pines, and other trees which grow in a Mediterranean climate, can be seen in the section of the arboretum nearest to the Maison Forestière.

Ⓑ Viewpoint. Looking across the extensive vineyards of the St. Phalès farmlands, and the pine-clad slopes of the rugged western ridge-tops of the Petit Lubéron.

Ⓒ Viewpoint looking along the upper section of the Ravin de Sabatier. Aromatic plants, Corsican pines and flowers make a heady scent in the hot sunshine, attracting multi-hued butterflies. Lizards and the occasional harmless snake may be seen sunning themselves on the rocks.

Ⓓ The white/red waymarks seen on this walk are for the GR6 – the *Alpes/Océan* long distance path (between pointers **❸** and **❼**), and the GR 97 near pointer **❼**, which follows the Durance valley.

Walk 14
VIEUX MÉRINDOL

6 km (3¾ miles)   Easy

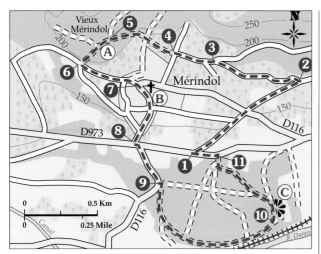

Vieux Mérindol sits on a hillock outside its 'modern' namesake. The 'new' village was built by survivors of religious persecution which wiped out the old village in the fourteenth century. Survivors and later incomers built their new village a little lower down the hillside to the south-east.

Mérindol is an attractive muddle of hidden ways and narrow streets which are centuries old. Traffic calming schemes in the centre have prevented the twentieth century from making too many inroads.

This walk is an excuse to wander around medieval highways and byways linked to a shaded woodland walk close to the River Durance. There are one or two modest restaurants and bars in the centre of Mérindol and a selection of shops you would expect to find in a self-sufficient village well away from any major town.

How to get there: Mérindol is on the D973 about half way between Cavaillon and Cadenet. Do not park in the centre of the village, but on the side road off the D973, next to the football ground east of the cemetery, where the walk starts and where there is usually ample space.

Route description

❶ Follow the side road north-east diagonally away from the main road. Go past a minor road on your left, then over a crossroads, gently uphill between olive groves and vineyards.

❷ Turn left along a level lane with an embankment on its right. Go past scattered houses, orchards and olive groves.

❸ Go half left, then half right at a staggered triple junction.

Continue ahead past several houses, two orchards and a vineyard to reach a T-junction.

❹ Go over the T-junction and ahead by a farm track beside a vineyard. Cross the next track and climb towards rough woodland bordering olive groves. Bear left with the track, past three or four houses.

❺ Go forwards at the next track junction, then fork left at the next, beside the ruins of Vieux Mérindol. Begin to go downhill.

❻ Turn left along the roadway, ignoring side turns, and continue with the road walking beside an embankment into the main village square and the church.

❼ Bear right from the church, gently downhill along the street as far as the main road.

❽ Cross the main road with care by going diagonally left to reach a side road. Follow this for about 330 metres, past a couple of side lanes on the left, and enter woodland.

❾ About 40 metres beyond a large house, turn left and immediately right on a woodland track. Follow it as it slowly swings to the left. Keep ahead at the next junction, and ignore other side tracks to your left. Walk down towards the riverside railway line and follow the embankment, ignoring two further side tracks, then go slightly uphill and away from the railway.

❿ Turn left at the track junction and left again at the next. Turn right at the next, then ahead past two further junctions. Bear right and join another track as far as the main road.

⓫ Turn left and follow the main road until you reach the football ground where the walk started.

Points of interest

Ⓐ Vieux Mérindol. Once the home of members of the heretical Vaudois sect who fled here from Italy in order to escape religious persecution. Mérindol was obliterated and all its inhabitants slaughtered by troops acting on the orders of Avignon popes in the fourteenth century. Foundations of a number of the old buildings have been excavated.

Ⓑ Many of the old houses lining Mérindol's central streets have been tastefully restored.

Ⓒ Viewpoint overlooking the Durance and its riverside fields and vineyards.

Walk 15
BUOUX

8 km (5 miles)   Easy/Moderate

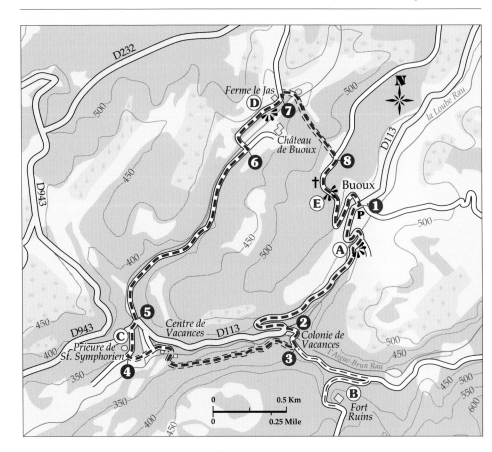

The D943 south from Apt to Lourmain climbs to the high wild limestone plateau connecting the Grand and Petit Lubéron hills. A side road, the D232, leaves the Apt road at its highest point, on the 499 metre (1637 ft) high Col de Pointu, and runs along the crest of a broad ridge where there is little or no habitation, to a remote crossroads. Here, a side turning on to the D113 follows a lavender-filled valley, into the almost medieval village of Buoux.

Below Buoux, a steep gorge sided by massive overhanging limestone cliffs flows down to its wooded valley bottom. It is here that monks built their secluded retreat, the Priory of St. Symphorien. A gentler woodland valley climbs out towards fertile upper slopes, past a partly restored château, from where farm tracks with distant views of lavender fields lead back to Buoux.

Buoux is only a quarter of an hour by car from Apt and the walk described here can fill a pleasant hour or two either late in the day, or when journeying to places in the south of Provençe.

Apt is the main town in the Lubéron area. It is built on Celto-Ligurian foundations, when it was called *Hath*. The Romans, when they took over, called their city *Apta Julia*. A busy town today, famous for crystallised fruits, its tiny central part still conveys the feel of medieval life. The church has served one of the oldest Christian communities. It was consecrated by Charlemagne, and is said to contain the relics of Ste. Anne, the mother of the Virgin Mary, which were brought from the Holy Land in AD776. As a result, Apt became a place of pilgrimage. In 1623 Anne of Austria prayed here for a child, a wish that was not granted for a further 15 years.

Lourmain is not far away, at the end of the D943 where it runs through the dramatic Combe de Bonnieux. Nearby is the cave which once housed notorious brigands, and the fifteenth century château has one of the prettiest courtyards in France. Albert Camus, the French winner of the Nobel Prize for Literature, and Henri Bosco, the Provençal novelist and poet, are both buried in the churchyard.

Buoux cannot aspire to any of the fame of its neighbours, but is all the better for it. A cluster of stone cottages and farmhouses that have stood the test of centuries, gaze out over an unchanging landscape. A place for quiet reflection and simple enjoyment.

There is one very good family-run restaurant, the Auberge de la Lube.

How to get there: Take the D943 south-east from Apt to the Col de Pointu. Go left on to the D232, then right at the crossroads with the D113 into Buoux. Alternatively, take the D113 all the way from Apt. There is a small car park next to the *Mairie,* one of the first buildings on entering Buoux from the north.

Route description

❶ Walk downhill along Buoux's single street, following the road as it winds beneath towering overhanging limestone cliffs, high above the deep wooded gorge on your left.

❷ Turn left in the valley bottom, along a side lane, past the *Colonie de Vacances.* Go over a bridge and, ignoring the riverside path to the right, go gently uphill to the second of two car parks, which should be on your right.

❸ Turn right on to a woodland path. Keeping well above the river, walk on until you reach the *Centre de Vacances.* Bear right away from the group of buildings, out along an access track.

❹ Turn right when you reach the road and go down to the river. Cross the bridge and turn left.

❺ Follow the narrow woodland side lane signposted to the Château de Buoux, uphill beneath the welcome shade of trees.

❻ Bear left where the road to the château goes forwards, cross over a bridge and make for the small farm of le Jas on the other side of the valley.

❼ Go past the main farm buildings, uphill for a little way, then right along a grassy track. Go past a small pond, then begin to go downhill through woodland overlooking Buoux.

❽ Bear right on reaching a surfaced farm access drive, zig-zagging with it downhill into Buoux.

Points of interest

Ⓐ Viewpoint over the high limestone cliffs bordering the Aigue Brun gorge. The area is a popular rock climbing venue.

Ⓑ An optional extension to the walk continues from route pointer **❸** by following signs pointing the way to a sixteenth-century hilltop fort, passing on the way the site of a Neolithic shelter beneath the overhanging rock. The hill fort was a Protestant stronghold during the Wars of Religion.

Ⓒ The tranquil, crumbling ruins of the Priory of St. Symphorien are unfortunately out of bounds for safety reasons, but you can view them from the surrounding wire fence.

Ⓓ Viewpoint. At the time of writing, Château de Buoux was undergoing restoration on behalf of the Lubéron National Park Authority. Check for details before visiting.

Ⓔ Viewpoint. Overlooking the rooftops of Buoux to lavender fields lining the upper valley of la Loube. Beyond, the land rises to the tree-clad heights of the Grand Lubéron.

Walk 16
MOURRE NÈGRE – THE GRAND LUBÉRON

12.5 km (7¾ miles)
Strenuous with 531 metres (1742ft) ascent

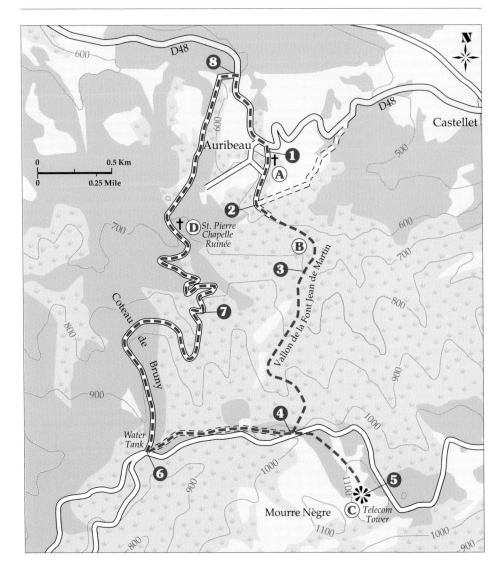

A long chain of interconnecting hills form an almost straight line, high to the south of the Calavon valley. Divided by Combe de Lourmain, where Bonnieux fits snugly below its col, the marginally lower hills to the west are called the Petit or 'Little' Lubéron. The range continues eastwards to the highest point, and is known as the Grand Lubéron. For centuries drovers used the freedom of these high summits to move sheep and cattle to the cities around the Rhône valley, or to the coast. Even now the tree line halts a few metres below the top of the ridge, not due to exposure to gales, but because it has traditionally been kept open to allow the passage of drove animals. A forest road winds its way along the ridge-top, following the footsteps of patient herds.

People living in villages along the foot of the Lubéron range are immensely proud of their region and its traditions. Many can trace their ancestry back to the fourteenth and sixteenth centuries when Protestants fled to these mountain hideaways in order to escape the bloody persecution of religious intolerance. The heretical Vaudois sect were pursued here from Italy, and by papal decree entire villages were wiped out.

Although the walk described here entails a fairly tough climb, the ascent is mostly under tree cover and therefore the heat need not be much of a problem. However, make sure you take sufficient drinks as there are no cafés for several miles!

The forests are the home of a wide variety of wildlife. Try to walk as quietly as possible and if you are lucky you might be rewarded by seeing roe deer, partridges or wild boar.

Auribeau, where the walk starts, is ancient. Set amongst lavender fields and with its back to the mountain, it offers a perfect vantage point for views of the nearby forests and mountain. There are no shops or bars in Auribeau.

How to get there: The D48 climbs from the town centre of Apt in a series of hairpin twists and turns, by way of Saignon. Alternatively, drive east from Apt along the N100 and turn right on to the other end of the D48, following it south-westwards through Castellet to reach Auribeau. Park at the roadside below the village.

Route description

❶ Climb up through the village and follow its narrow alleyways, past stone-built cottages and its venerable church. Follow the lane beyond the church, along the edge of an escarpment. Cross a road end and go to the left of the cemetery, downhill along a narrow lane and above a series of now tree-covered ancient terraces.

❷ Where the surfaced track turns sharp left, go forwards and uphill on a steadily roughening track, between two separate modern houses. The track narrows to a footpath. Follow it still uphill and into the forest, swinging around the steep hillside, then downhill a little way into the densely wooded side valley of Vallon de la Font Jean de Martin. Begin the steep climb up the narrow woodland gorge.

❸ Ignoring any side paths, follow the valley bottom steadily uphill, leaving the usually dry stream bed by swinging left with the path up the start of a final spur which leads to the ridge-crest.

❹ Cross a forestry road and climb the now open grassy hillside to the telecom tower marking the summit of Mourre Nègre.

❺ Retrace the upward path as far as the forestry road at route pointer ❹ and turn left, following the track downhill into the forest.

❻ Turn sharp right beside a water tank marking the complex junction of tracks and forest roads, and follow the unsurfaced forest road down, then around the tree-clad hillside spur of Coteau de Bruny, then around the zig-zag turns.

❼ Avoid any tempting short cuts between the bends. They save very little time, cause erosion and are more tiring. Continue to follow the track downhill until it reaches the main road.

❽ Turn right and follow the road the short distance between a series of fields into Auribeau.

Points of interest

Ⓐ Viewpoint. Auribeau's church makes an ideal vantage point for views of the nearby mountain and its forested slopes.

Ⓑ Woodland flowers such as orchids and anemones bloom in late spring, followed later by rare cyclamens. Amongst the strange wildlife on the mountainside you might be fortunate to find lizard-like salamanders in damp crevices amongst the rocks.

Ⓒ Viewpoint. To the north of the summit of Mourre Nègre the view looks down on to the Calavon valley where an abandoned railwayline has been converted into a car-free cycleway between Apt and Forcalquier. Beyond the valley are the rolling hills of the Lubéron National Park. Southwards, and on a clear day, you can see the almost alpine hills above Aix, and beyond, the sparkle of the Mediterranean and the Camargue.

Ⓓ A little to the right of the track, and almost hidden in the trees, the poignant ruins of the Chapelle St. Pierre stand on a rounded hillock.

Walk 17
REILLANNE

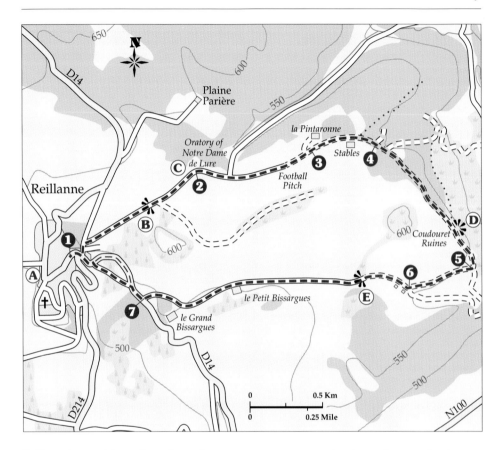

Reillanne is one of those places that makes no attempt to attract tourists, but at the same time it opens its welcoming arms to anyone who chances to drive along the plane tree shaded access from the N100. Arriving in its split-level square the visitor might feel alone until eye to eye contact is rewarded by the friendliest of smiles.

It might seem that Reillanne's one moment of glory is the annual cheese festival held every May, after which the village might be expected to go to sleep again. This is far from the truth, for Reillanne has a thriving community spirit which welcomes everyone who takes an interest in its affairs. If, when you park, there are small boys and maybe their elders playing *boule,* watch out for your ankles because somehow or other the direction of play will almost certainly come your way. A bit of light-hearted bantering in *franglais* will result in grins all round.

The lovely old village sprawls across a complex valley head. Narrow terraced vineyards climb the hillsides and the highest ground is covered by pinewoods.

To the north of Reillanne, the massive convent of Notre-Dame is hidden in dense forest at the end of a long winding track beyond the village.

One might expect to find an observatory in St. Michel-l'Observatoire, the next village on the far side of the Largue valley to the north-east of Reillanne. Once a fortified town (there are still a few traces of the outer walls) all that remains of its former glory is a pleasing number of medieval houses. However, a side road from St. Michel, the D305, does lead to a real observatory. This is the Observatory of Haute Provençe which opens its doors to visitors on advertised days in summer. An interesting place to visit, details of opening times can be obtained at the Tourist Office in Forcalquier.

Céreste is another interesting place to the west of Reillanne. The modern N100 cuts through the centre, following a winding path between the relics of its outer defences. A winding rural side road leads over to the ravine-like valley of the Carluc, where a priory stands by the remains of an early Christian necropolis carved from the rock.

The walk explores the gentle farming countryside to the east of Reillanne, using softly undulating tracks and footpaths amidst ever-changing vistas. As you would expect from a village at the heart of a farming community, Reillanne has plenty to offer in the way of good, but unpretentious bars and small family-run restaurants. There are also a useful number of produce shops and bakeries.

How to get there: Approaching from the direction of Apt (from the west), a tree-shaded dual-laned side road, the D214 (the Apt to Forcalquier road), leads directly into the centre of Reillanne. Alternatively, if travelling from the direction of Forcalquier, turn right to follow the D14 into the village. Park in either the upper or lower part of the split level square.

Route description

❶ Follow the D14 east away from the square, across the head of a steep side valley, then take the first turning on your left. Follow this lane to the second turning on the right, and turn right to follow the direction of the signpost pointing to the Stade (football pitch).

❷ Bear right with the lane as it passes a wayside shrine. Ignore the next turning left into a shallow valley, but walk on towards, then past the football pitch.

❸ Walk forwards beyond the football ground, on an unsurfaced track, past riding stables and into scrub woodland.

❹ Take the right fork at the next three track junctions and go over a gradually rising hill. Go downhill past two separate ruins with the woodland boundary on your left.

❺ Turn sharp right at a track junction, uphill above a series of terraces and past a small barn.

❻ Bear right where the track joins a farm lane beside a couple of farm buildings. Follow its gradually improving surface, over a wooded rise, then gradually downhill between vines and open fields. Go past two farmhouses and, using the church tower in Reillanne for direction, head towards the village.

❼ Turn right when you reach the road, following either its old or modern route into Reillanne. Both are tree shaded and go past interesting houses.

Points of interest

Ⓐ Explore the lovely old village either before or after the walk. Its ancient high-walled church and separate triple-belled tower is well worth the climb from the lower village.

Ⓑ Viewpoint. Pause to look back at the photogenic view of Reillanne with the older part of the village climbing high above the encircling vines.

Ⓒ The wayside shrine, the Oratory of Notre Dame de Lure, was erected in 1806 by a local as an offering of thanks for an apparently miraculous cure.

Ⓓ Viewpoint looking east towards Haute Provençe and the Basse Alpes, close to the Franco-Italian border.

Ⓔ A 'Surprise View' of Reillanne appears ahead, and of the Lubéron Hills to the left, when the track leaves a small belt of woodland.

Walk 18
COL DE L'AIRE DEÏ MASCO

5 km (3 miles)   Moderate

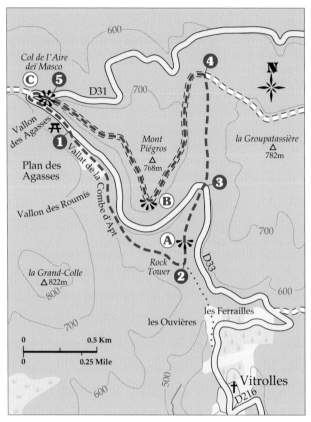

Route description

❶ Walk downstream along the woodland path from the picnic site, following yellow waymarks.

❷ Turn left at the path junction beside a rock tower. Climb steeply uphill beside a dry stream bed, ignoring side paths to the left.

❸ Cross the road and continue steeply uphill on the stony path opposite. Climb the dry wooded valley.

❹ Turn left on joining a forest track, following an easier gradient uphill, around the spur of the forested hillside of Mt Piégros, then follow the contours before starting to go downhill.

❺ Turn left on reaching the road. Follow it round the tight left-hand bend and go downhill to the picnic site.

Points of interest

Ⓐ Viewpoint looking south towards vineyards surrounding the tiny village of Vitrolles. Beyond them, and in the hazy distance across the Durance valley, are the rugged outlines of the Alpes Maritimes.

Ⓑ Viewpoint. Golden eagles, buzzards and other birds of prey are frequent visitors to these arid forests. At ground level lizards scurry away in a flash on your approach. Scorpions can often be found in cool pockets under flat stones. They have an undeserved reputation, but do not torment them. They will not deliberately attack, but can sting in self defence. While not normally lethal, a scorpion sting can be very painful indeed.

Ⓒ Viewpoint. The Col de l'Aire Deï Masco has spectacular views to the north towards the Calavon valley and south across the Durance towards high limestone hills surrounding Aix-en-Provence.

No major roads cross the Lubéron range, but several minor roads link the Calavon and Durance valleys. Crossing an easterly spur of the Grand Lubéron, the D31 climbs in a series of tight hairpins south from Céreste to a high col where it becomes the D33.

The walk follows woodland ways, and starts from a forest picnic site beside the D33 where it descends steeply to the unspoilt village of Vitrolles and the Durance plain.

There are no refreshments available nearby, so take a picnic. Using a path beside the usually dry river bed of the Vallat de la Combe d'Apt, the stiffest part of the walk begins next to a group of strangely worn limestone towers. Once out of the confines of the side valleys, the walking is much easier, following a contour-hugging track where birds of prey soar on the hot rising air.

How to get there: Take the D31/D33 south from the N100 via Céreste. Or go north-east from Pertuis (D973) on the D956 to Grambois and then take the D33 north. The picnic site is signposted from the D33 about 380 metres (415yds) below the col.

Walk 19
MIRABEAU

4 km (2½ miles)   Easy

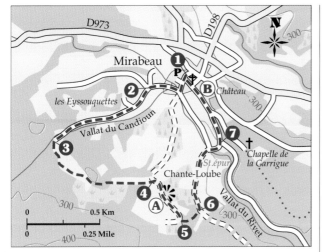

Filling the odd hour or so between venues, this short stroll is around the pretty village of Mirabeau. On no tourist itineraries, it lies in a sunny hollow high above the bustle of autoroute traffic following the Durance to Aix road and beyond.

A venerable old château overlooks the day-to-day events in the village, and has been lived in by the same family for generations. To the north of Mirabeau, the land rises steadily through the rolling forested hills to the giant whaleback of the Lubéron chain. It is a mysterious place where persecuted so-called heretics found sanctuary in the Middle Ages, building their fortress villages on impregnable mounds. The Knights Templars, a military order founded in 1118 to protect pilgrims travelling to the Holy Land, had a fortress a little to the north of Mirabeau. Along with other castles belonging to the order, it was suppressed in 1312 by Philip IV, who coveted their wealth and growing power.

There are a couple of small but excellent medium-priced restaurants near the square below the church.

How to get there: Even though Mirabeau is well hidden from the main valley, it is easy to reach. Leave the N96 above the Pont Mirabeau across the River Durance and follow the D973 (the hill road to Pertuis) to a short side road on the left. Park in the Place de la Fontaine near the post office, the PTT.

Route description

1 The walk starts in front of the church. With your back to the church turn left to walk downhill along a narrow side lane leading towards scattered groups of modern houses. Go past two side turnings, right and left, then down to a crossroads in the valley bottom and turn right. Walk uphill past old and new houses.

2 Turn left at the staggered crossroads and, ignoring a side turning on the right after a little over 100 metres, follow the country lane along the valley side and into open country.

3 Where the surfaced lane ends, turn left and uphill. Ignoring side turnings into fields and old properties, walk on between tiny meadows and small vineyards, in and out of rough woodland, over rising ground then down to a series of larger vineyards.

4 Turn right and uphill on joining a rough surfaced track, past old vineyards.

5 Where the lane wings hard to the right, go to the left, downhill along a woodland path.

6 Turn left at the junction with a cart track. Go downhill between vines, then ahead at the next junction, and cross to the other side of the valley.

7 Go to the left on joining the old valley bottom road. Walk uphill along it, beneath the walls of the château and back to the village.

Points of interest

A Viewpoint. Across the broad headwaters of the Vallat du Rivet, the old houses of Mirabeau still cluster for protection around the time-mellowed walls of the fortress-like château.

B Time spent exploring Mirabeau's winding alleys and back lanes will be rewarded by the discovery of half-hidden statues of long dead notables, and tiny flower-filled cottage gardens.

Walk 20
FORÊT DOMANIALE DE
CORBIÈRES   7.5 km (3¾ miles)   Easy/ Moderate

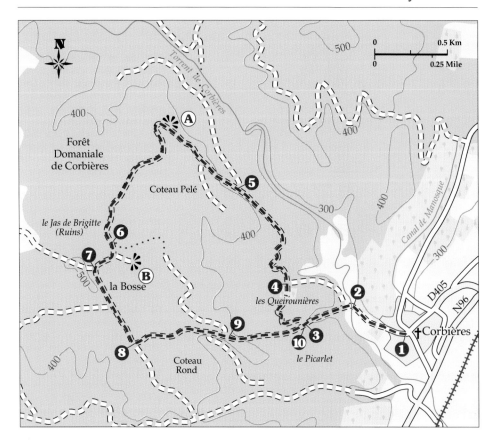

People living in Corbières have the traditional right to hunt game and remove timber from the forest-clad slopes to the west of the village. This traditional right is centuries old, stemming from the days when the necessity of finding both fuel and extra meat involved more than picking up the telephone, or nipping down to the local supermarket. That right is still jealously guarded and although modern commercial timber cutting is carefully controlled, hunting continues, although it is more of a social event during the winter months.

Even though there is a moderate climb at the start, the walk is mainly in natural woodland, and so escapes the glare and heat of the Provençal sunshine.

Wildlife abounds, especially forest dwelling birds, and by walking quietly it is possible to come across roe deer and maybe families of wild boar *(sanglier)*. The latter lead a hectic life during the hunting season, being considered a great delicacy. Potentially dangerous only if provoked, wild boar should be treated with respect.

Manosque is the nearest town of note, about nine kilometres (5¹/₂ miles) to the north-east along the N96. A commercial centre, handling fruit and vegetable produce from the fertile borders of the River

Durance, Manosque was built in the fourteenth century. Those strange woodland delicacies, truffles, are still marketed here, not in modern warehouses, but by semi-clandestine meetings where deals are on a strictly cash-only basis.

King François Ist entered the town through the Porte Saunerie, one of two town gates which still restrict traffic in and out of the oldest part of the town. He was given the keys of the town by the mayor's pretty daughter who caught the king's eye, and he made it known that he wished to exercise his right of *droite de seigneur*. This so horrified the poor girl's father that he promptly threw acid into her face, disfiguring her for life, but saving her from the lecherous hands of the king.

St. Sauveur's church in the town centre is topped by a wrought iron belfry. Erected in the eighteenth century, campaniles such as this are a common feature throughout Provençe, and are known as 'God's sheep bells'.

Downstream from Corbières is the Cadarache Nuclear Power Station, close to the confluence of the Verdon with the Durance.

In early spring, or after prolonged heavy rain, the Torrent de Corbières lives up to its literal translation into English. In summer the stream dries to a mere trickle and the walk fords it by a concrete slipway very near the start (see route pointer ❷). If you have been unlucky with the weather and it has been raining hard for several days, then it is possible you may not be able to ford the stream dry-shod. It is therefore suggested that you leave this attractive walk for a drier day.

Corbières has a number of small bars and restaurants together with a useful selection of boulangeries and pâtisseries if you want to make up a picnic.

How to get there: The N96 Durance valley road to Aix-en-Provence skirts Corbières, nine kilometres (5¹/₂ miles) south-west of Manosque. Park in the centre of the village near the church and post office, PTT.

Route description

❶ Behind the church the narrow Rue des Gabians leads downhill, past cottages and out towards riverside meadows. Ignore a lane to the left beyond the last house and follow what becomes a cart track, down to the stream.

❷ Cross the ford by the concrete spillway and climb the opposite bank. Turn left at the first track junction and climb fairly steeply beside a narrow side valley and into woodland.

❸ Turn right at the fork and follow the track below a series of old terraces to cross the side valley and go through a small orchard.

❹ Go over the track junction above more terraces, then down into, and across a second side valley. Climb fairly steeply through forest and up the terraced hillside.

❺ Bear left at the track junction and ignore a second left junction after about 350 metres, still uphill through dense forest, then on easier levels as the track swings left around the upper slopes of the Coteau Pelé to reach a broad col.

❻ Ignore a narrow downhill path on the left, and walk on for another 90 metres or so, then turn left to climb a little way to the summit of la Bosse. Return to the track junction at route pointer ❻ and turn left downhill to another col.

❼ Go over the track junction and then bear left steadily downhill. Ignore a further track to the right and walk on through the forest and begin to go slightly uphill and around a small rise.

❽ Turn sharp left at the next track junction, steeply downhill beside a small stream bed. Go over an adjoining stream and bear right along the fairly level track and away from the stream. Ignore the track on the right, continuing downstream. Go forwards and up to the side ridge.

❾ Join another track coming from your left and go downhill on the far side of the ridge, diagonally right across the forested hillside.

❿ Go ahead at the next track junction to walk downhill along part of the outward track as far as the river. Cross the ford and follow the field track, and then the roadway, into Corbières.

Points of interest

Ⓐ Viewpoint. Across the steeply cut valley of the Torrent de Corbières, you should be able to make out some of the narrow twists and turns of the hill road which serves farms on the upper plateau. This road is known as the *Piste du Trou du Loup*, the 'Road of the Wolf's Lair'. It is unlikely you will find wolves in this part of France nowadays, but you might see wild boar and deer.

Ⓑ Viewpoint. Forest trees attractively frame the view across the Durance valley.

Walk 21
FORCALQUIER

6 km (3¾ miles)   Easy/Moderate

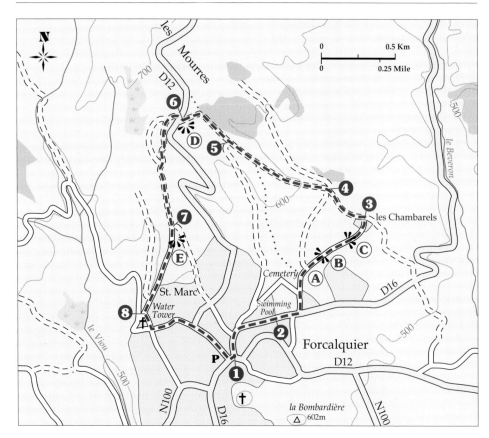

Forcalquier makes an ideal base for anyone exploring central Provençe. To its north the land rises steadily across a seemingly barren waste of limestone terraces, but where exquisitely coloured flowers prove that the landscape is far from bare. The land continues to rise until it reaches the summit ridge of the Montagne de Lure, where the highest point, the Signal de Lure at 1,826 metres (5,991ft), must be reached on foot. Closer to hand, and at the end of a long side road to the west of Forcalquier, is the Observatory of Haute Provence. Open on advertised days, a visit to the observatory opens up the mysteries of the universe; but even if this does not interest you very much, a visit is worthwhile if only to enjoy the lovely setting.

In the Middle Ages Forcalquier was known as *Furnus Calcarius,* from the number of lime kilns around the town. The modern name is a direct descent from the Latin. King Henry III of England's marriage to Eleanore of Provençe in 1235 is commemorated by a fifteenth-century fountain in front of the church of Notre Dame. At the time of the marriage of King Henry to Eleanore, Forcalquier was the capital of a large part of Haute-Provençe. Once the seat of counts, it was famous for its court where Provençal troubadours entertained the guests.

The view of Forcalquier on the approach from Apt (on the N100) is of a tall basilica church and a citadel overtopping the oldest part of the town. Red-roofed houses of all shapes and sizes seem to cascade towards what looks like more level ground, where the modern part of Forcalquier stands. Nearby is a well-restored Franciscan monastery. Founded in 1236, it is one of the earliest Franciscan orders in France. The monastery is open to visitors, and a walk round the cloisters is especially rewarding. There was once a large Jewish community in Forcalquier, but all that is left is the synagogue in the old quarter of the town.

Like most French rural towns, market days are colourful affairs. The square in front of Notre Dame church is filled with stalls selling local produce as well as everyday essentials. Music festivals are held most years during the summer months.

About a kilometre from the town centre, and passed on this walk, is one of the oddest tourist attractions imaginable. This is the town's cemetery which is visited by coach parties from far and wide. Terraces lined with carefully tended yew hedges border immaculately kept graves alongside more elaborate cabanes (small, cylindrical drystone mausoleums with pointed roofs).

The walk sets out into open country to the north-east of the town, before climbing gradually to the area known as les Mourres, where limestone outcrops and natural terraces are filled with aromatic shrubs and sub-alpine flowers of every imaginable hue. Returning trackways offer dramatic views of the old town of Forcalquier on top of its towering hill.

Forcalquier is large enough to support every form of eating place from simple pizza parlours to three-star restaurants. There is also a wide range of shops.

How to get there: From the N96 Aix road through the Durance valley take the D13 north-west from Volx near Manosque. If travelling south along the N96, turn west off along the D12 beyond Peyruis. Alternatively follow the N100 east from the direction of Apt, direct to Forcalquier. Park in the town centre.

Route description

❶ From the marketplace in the town centre, follow side streets and signposts pointing to the *piscine* (municipal open-air swimming pool).

❷ Go past the swimming pool and sports complex and turn left along a side lane leading towards the cemetery and out into open country. Head towards the prominent group of buildings which make up the hamlet of les Chambarels.

❸ Go past the first houses and turn left at the T-junction in les Chambarels. Follow a cart track out between tiny fields and scrub woodland.

❹ Keep ahead at the four-way track crossing.

❺ Go ahead, where another track joins climbing from the left. Climb through rocky outcrops below a sparsely tree-covered hill marking the start of the limestone desert of les Mourres. Make for a small group of roadside houses.

❻ Cross the road by going diagonally right, then half left along a side lane between farm buildings. Swing more to the left and begin to go downhill.

❼ Bear right at the fork, taking the downhill track.

❽ Turn left at a complex junction beside a small chapel. Walk downhill on the road and past the front of a battlemented water tower, then go first left, then right to make your way into the town centre.

Points of interest

Ⓐ The official entrance to the cemetery is from the road to your left, but the best view of the topiaried yew hedges is by looking back a little further and uphill along the walk.

Ⓑ Viewpoint. Again looking back towards the dramatic hilltop site of old Forcalquier, together with its basilica and fortress château.

Ⓒ Viewpoint. On a clear day, looking east you can see the foothills of the Alps, way beyond the high limestone plateaux of Haute-Provençe.

Ⓓ Viewpoint. The old town still looks impregnable no matter what aspect it is viewed from. Closer to hand, or more correctly at foot, the outcropping arid limestone desert known as les Mourres is full of aromatic shrubs such as rosemary, lavender and juniper, as well as scores of different varieties of sub-alpine flowers. Brightly coloured butterflies hover around the nectar filled flower heads, and lizards disappear in a flash as you approach their sunbeds.

Ⓔ Viewpoint. Beyond the descending track, a further aspect of Forcalquier opens to the south.

Walk 22
ST. ETIENNE LES ORGUES

6 km (3¾ miles)   Easy

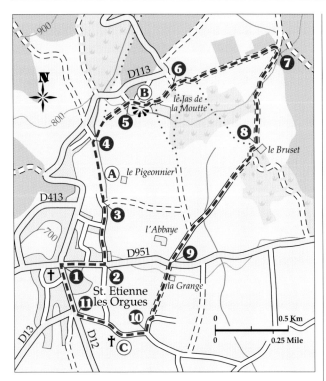

The D113 climbs out of the town, climbing northwards in a series of tight, exciting twists and turns, through dense natural oak and pine forests to cross the long ridge of the Montagne de Lure. The Lure hills are really an extension of Mont Ventoux to the west. They form an almost continuous chain of limestone hills, sheltering the rest of Provence from the effects of cold air drawn from the Alps further north. Streams vanish abruptly into caves (*dolines*) in the limestone rocks, re-appearing in the lower valleys after wandering an unknown distance underground. Even though the road passes within a comparatively short distance of the summit, to reach the top of the Signal de Lure – 1826 m (5991ft) – it is necessary to walk up the final steep path from the road. Fortunately there is a small refreshment hut when you get there. From the viewing platform, on a clear day, breathtaking views taking in most of the south-western corner of the Alps, and many summits above the 4,000 metre contour, can be seen. Rare alpine flowers, such as St. Bruno's lilies, gentians, cushion saxifrages and snake's-head fritillaries, bloom in hidden folds between the rocks once the last snows of winter have melted.

A side turning off the road to the Montagnes de Lure, a mile or two above St. Etienne, leads downwards from the oratory of St. Joseph, through the pinewoods to the Lure

St. Etienne sits at the foot of scrub and pine-clad rolling hills, side ridges of the Montagne de Lure range to its north. To the south, lavender fields fill the air with their heady perfume. Out-of-town modern developments in no way detract from the attractions of the old village and its market square.

During the Middle Ages, St. Etienne became famous for its medicines and quack remedies. These were based on herbal preparations handed down by word of mouth since the earliest times; in fact many of the locals still swear by ancient family potions made from the herbs which grow in the surrounding meadows and woodlands.

The name of the town St. Etienne les Orgues suggests connections with some form of organ pipes; *orgues* means 'organ', but apart from the attractive instrument used to accompany hymn singing in the village church, there is no history of organ-making; neither are there any organ-pipe rock formations nearby in this predominantly limestone area. The controversy is further compounded by the fact that some maps even drop les Orgues, preferring to simply call the place St. Etienne.

46

Hermitage. A small Romanesque chapel, founded in AD500 by St. Donat, now stands on the site.

From a crossroads below the oldest part of St. Etienne, farm lanes and grassy paths explore the ancient field patterns and quiet meadows of this secluded backwater.

As a modest holiday resort, St. Etienne has a good selection of friendly bars, small family-run restaurants and pizza parlours, as well as a good range of pâtisserie, boulangerie and charcutier shops.

How to get there: From Forcalquier, take the narrow D12 over the magnificent 'moon-like' landscape of the limestone wilderness of les Mourres. This route takes you through a series of tiny villages and leads directly to St. Etienne les Orgues centre. Alternatively, the D951 can be used if travelling south along the Durance valley. This road leaves the N99 at the tiny village of Peipin and travels west by way of St. Donat les Chabannes.

Route description

❶ From the traffic-calming cobbles of the town centre, follow the D951 Cruis road eastwards to the outskirts.

❷ Turn left at a crossroads, opposite a wayside cross. Walk steadily uphill, following the side lane, past occasional properties and on into open fields, ignoring any side turnings.

❸ Where the lane forks beside a shallow, probably dried up little stream, continue ahead to follow the field path closest to the left of the stream.

❹ Reaching the edge of a modern housing development, turn right and cross the stream bed. Walk steadily uphill and go to the right when the path joins a cart track.

❺ Turn right at the cross tracks on the corner of woodland. Walk towards the farm of le Jas de la Moutte. Bear left with the track as it passes the entrance to the farm. Climb beside woodland.

❻ Take the right fork at the track junction to cross the hillside, then go gently downhill along the edge of two sections of woodland and into the rocky bed of a winter-flowing stream.

❼ Turn sharp right away from the stream bed and go downhill away from the forest. Bear left along the edge of a plantation and then go between two more, heading steadily downhill towards the farmhouse of le Bruset.

❽ Follow an access lane to your right, away from le Bruset. Continue downhill between fields on a steadily improving roadway. Ignore all side turnings until you reach the main road.

❾ Go past a little shrine and cross the D951 road. Follow a side lane beside the farm of la Grange and between fields. The lane later joins a better surfaced road. Continue along it to a gap in the terraced hillside masking a T-junction.

❿ Turn right along the minor road, following it below the embankment, past a wayside shrine and continue towards the outskirts of St. Etienne.

⓫ Go to the right at the five-ways junction and follow the main road from Forcalquier into the centre of St. Etienne.

Points of interest

Ⓐ The tower-like building to your right across the fields is based on an ancient *pigeonnier*, or pigeon cote. The birds were encouraged to roost here for two purposes. Not only was pigeon meat a handy and attractive addition to the diet when winter-killed meat had been used up, but pigeon droppings were a useful source of rich fertiliser. The inside of the *pigeonnier* was arranged so that a ladder mounted on a turntable could be used for easy access to the birds' nests.

Ⓑ Viewpoint looking south over the village to the dry limestone hills leading to Forcalquier. The dry sandy soil in the broad, almost water-free valley on the far side of St. Etienne les Orgues, makes an ideal environment for lavender growing.

Ⓒ Wayside shrines, oratories and tiny crosses are attractive landmarks that you see frequently when walking in France and other Catholic countries. Often decorated with bright posies, they are often built on the site of wayside preaching crosses which date from the time when Christianity was preached to a heathen population.

Walk 23

BANON AND THE RUINED VILLAGE OF HAUT MONSALIER

10 km (6 miles)   Moderate/ Strenuous
146 metres (479ft) Climb

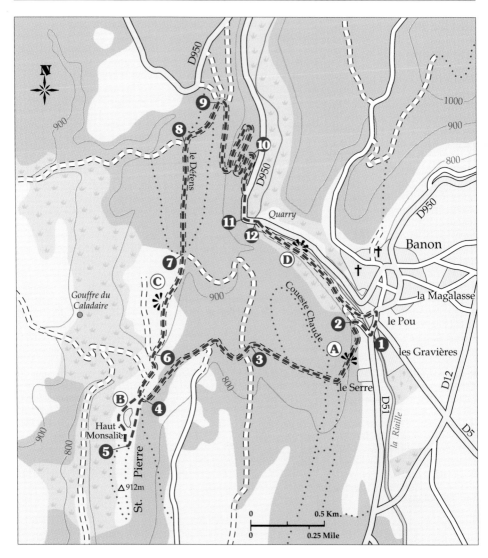

Ancient cottages line the narrow streets of Banon, which is surrounded by starkly wooded hillsides and lush pastures. The sad remains of the long-abandoned village of Haut Monsalier stand on a high narrow ridge looking out across the lowlands. This is the high point of the walk in more sense than one. Not far away, and in complete contrast, is the Gouffre du Caladaire, at 480 metres (1,575 feet) deep, one of the deepest cave systems in France.

Banon's main industry is quarrying limestone, but it also prides itself on the quality of its cheeses. Every year a festival, the *Fête de Fromage*, is held at the end of May in homage of the local cheese industry. Cheeses of all sizes and textures are displayed in hotly competed classes.

Banon has the requisite number of restaurants, bars and shops to cope with inner needs at the end of this fairly tough walk.

Starting in the normally dry valley bottom of the River Raille, a steep, but well-made track climbs the scrub-covered hillside, crossing a couple of side spurs before reaching the narrow ridge of St. Pierre. Here, on its very crest, stands the abandoned village of Haut Monsalier. The ridge is followed past medieval field systems to the main hillside of le Défens where a zig-zag track returns to the valley bottom.

How to get there: Banon is at the junction of the D51 road climbing north from the Calavon valley by way of Simiane-la-Rotonde and the D950 Forcalquier to Sault road, along with the D14/D5 north from Reillanne and Vachères. Parking space is limited in the town centre, but can usually be found near the group of houses at le Pou around the junction of the D51 and D5 in the valley bottom below Banon.

Route description

1 From the road junction at le Pou, cross the bridge and turn right along a side track, past houses and a group of small industrial buildings.

2 Turn left on the rough track climbing the scrub and scree-covered hillside. Bear right around the top of a side ridge.

3 Bear left to cross a small dry stream bed and go ahead at cross tracks, then over another side valley. Take the right fork at the next junction and begin to climb more steeply, bearing left up the scrub-covered hillside.

4 Go to the left of a complex track junction and out along the open ridge-top to reach the ruined village.

5 Turn sharp right at the far end of the ruins and follow a path a little below the ruins and along the rim of the ridge, back to the track junction at route pointer **4** . Continue ahead and begin to climb a broader part of the ridge. Bear slightly to your right where a side track descends on the left. Ignoring other descending side tracks, continue uphill.

6 Take the right fork and, still climbing, go through a series of old field systems and towards the woodland boundary ahead of you.

7 Walk ahead over the cross tracks on the forest boundary and gently go uphill.

8 Follow the track around the forested hillside beyond a junction with another track climbing from the left. Ignore any minor tracks to the right and left. Follow the main, well-used track.

9 Go sharply to the right at a complex track junction, gradually downhill at first, then steeply zig-zagging through four tight bends.

10 Walk parallel with the road for a little way, then join it.

11 Follow the road round the sharp left-hand corner and go over the bridge.

12 Turn right below the bridge, following the side track to cross the dry river bed. Following its bank, walk downstream back by way of the small industrial area into le Pou.

Points of interest

A Viewpoint. The once fortified village of Banon seems to cling precariously to the hillside, but has stood the test of time and enemies since the Saracens came marauding and pillaging this way in the Middle Ages.

B The abandoned village of Haut Monsalier. There are conflicting stories about the demise of this village. One story says it was destroyed by papal decree during the Wars of Religion in the Middle Ages. Another says its inhabitants died of bubonic plague when it ravaged Europe in the mid-fourteenth century, temporarily halting the Hundred Years War. However, the remains look a little too recent to be medieval and one must suspect its isolated position led to the inhabitants of Haut Monsalier abandoning it in favour of somewhere more convenient. Whatever the reason, the hilltop situation lends the place a certain romantic aura.

C Viewpoint. At the foot of the hill and on the edge of the forest, the Gouffre du Caladaire is one of the deepest and most extensive cave systems in France. Cave explorers have determined its initial depth as being over 480 metres (1,575 feet).

D Viewpoint. The especially hard limestone dug out from the quarry makes excellent building material.

Walk 24
JOUQUES

7 km (4¼ miles)   Easy

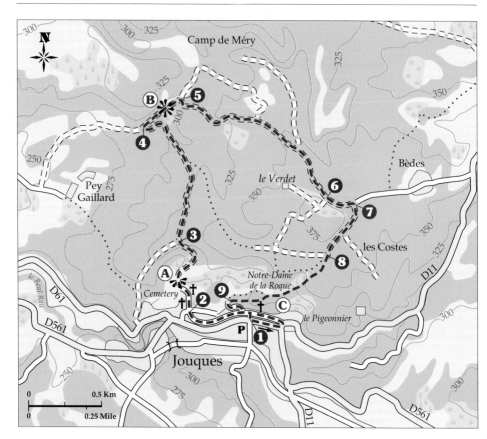

The rolling hills which overlook the Durance valley to the north-east of Aix-en-Provence are often missed in favour of better-known attractions. Jouques therefore comes as something of a surprise. Set amongst the tree-clad hills, the pleasant little town faces south across a narrow green valley. Well away from the noise of traffic thundering down the Autoroute du Val Durance, Jouques has the air of a turn-of-the-century resort. Known only to those who have discovered its charms, the town is well worth the short diversion east from the Durance valley. No longer linked to the rest of Provence by the quaint little train that used to puff its way along the main valley at Peyrolles, you almost feel that with the demise of steam, Jouques simply abandoned all hope of becoming a major holiday resort.

The walk climbs rapidly above Jouques, then rambles by quiet woodland paths within sight of the Durance valley, but fortunately out of earshot of its traffic. On the return, a short diversion is made to visit an attractive old hilltop chapel.

In keeping with its one-time splendour, the town still boasts one or two good restaurants as well as more moderate priced cafés and bars. There is also a good selection of food shops.

How to get there: Jouques is at the junction of the D61 and D561 in the Real valley about five kilometres (3 miles) uphill to the east of Peyrolles-en-Provence. Park in the centre of the town in the Place des Ancien Combatants.

Route description

❶ Turn right away from the car park and riverside gardens and follow the main street to the T-junction at its far end. Turn left, then almost immediately left again to follow backstreets generally uphill and roughly parallel to the main street. Bear right, still uphill, to reach the parish church.

❷ Go over a crossroads next to the church and follow the narrow lane on the right of the cemetery wall. Begin to go steadily uphill again , bearing right then left past a group of houses and a wayside shrine. Ignore the track on your left and climb the short but steep vine-terraced dry valley. Follow what becomes a cart track through a gap in the outcropping line of limestone crags. Walk on into scrub oak and pine woodland.

❸ Bear right at the track junction and start to go steadily downhill along the shady woodland track.

❹ Turn right on joining a slightly wider track, uphill past small tree-sheltered vineyards opposite a ruined farmhouse.

❺ Turn sharp right at the track junction and still climbing, walk on past the next two tracks joining from the left, then along level ground.

❻ Bear slightly left at a track junction below the open hilltop and go downhill.

❼ Where the track joins a surfaced road, turn immediately to your right, along another forest track. Follow the track around, then down the higher ground, past an old woodland cottage. Ignoring a lesser track deviating to your left, go a little more steeply downhill.

❽ Where the forest track turns sharply to your right, take the far left of two converging paths, downhill beside a narrow line of terraced stony vineyards, then climb the rocky scrub-covered hillock topped by the ancient chapel. Go forwards away from the chapel, downhill towards the upper part of Jouques.

❾ On reaching the first houses, bear left, then right, downhill along the backstreets to reach the town centre.

Points of interest

Ⓐ Viewpoint overlooking Jouques and the rolling hilltop forests towards the distant pinnacle of la Croix de Provence, the highest point of Mont Ste. Victoire which overlooks Aix-en-Provençe.

Ⓑ Viewpoint looking north-east along the valley of the Durance. Opposite across the valley, a long dark forested ridge marks the centre of the Lubéron National Park.

Ⓒ Viewpoint. The oratory chapel of Notre-Dame de la Roque has beckoned travellers across the mountainous plateau for centuries.

Walk 25
REFUGE CÉZANNE

9 km (5½ miles)   Moderate

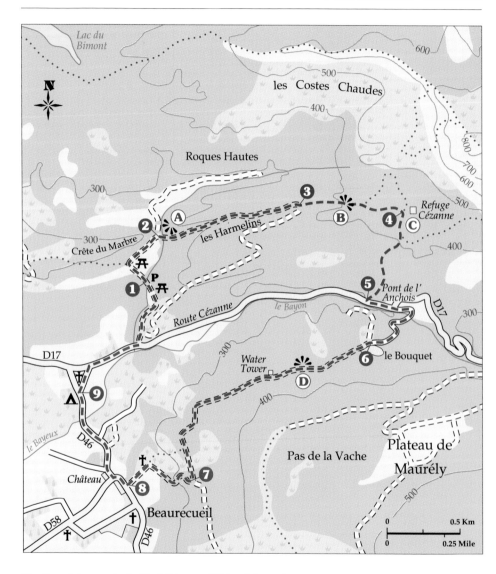

The French impressionist Paul Cézanne (1839-1906) was born at nearby Aix, and found much of his inspiration as an artist around the foothills of Mont Ste. Victoire. Overlooking Aix, the mountain takes its name from a famous Roman victory over the invading Teuton hordes.

High limestone crags, the province of rock climbers and alpinists, fall dramatically to the south of this 945m (3100ft) mountain. On its summit the Croix de Provençe commands a view overlooking the Mediterranean and the Alps as far as the Dauphiné in the north.

Cézanne's link with the mountain is commemorated by a mountain hut at the foot of the south face of Mont Ste. Victoire. The Refuge Cézanne opens its doors to all who seek the beauty and solitude of the mountain and is the focal point of this walk. Rolling foothills, so loved by Cézanne, are explored on a walk where every turn brings fresh delight. Even though it wanders close to the preserve of the skilled rock climber, the walk is safe and uses broad, well-graded paths throughout.

Being situated at the highest point of the walk, the Refuge Cézanne makes an ideal stopping place. It is normally open throughout the summer months and offers a wide range of simple, but palatable fare. Check beforehand if you intend to rely upon it for refreshment, but in any case it is wiser to carry at least a bottle of water as there are few other opportunities for a drink.

Strong footwear is essential on this walk.

How to get there: Take the D17 east from Aix by way of le Tholonet, where the old mill was frequently one of Cézanne's subjects. Go past the junction with the D46 Châteauneuf-le-Rouge road, and drive on for a little over 450 metres (quarter of a mile). Cross a road bridge and immediately turn left uphill on a concrete road signposted to the Domaine Roques Hautes. The road soon becomes a sandy track which leads into a picnic site and car parking area where the walk starts.

Route description

❶ Follow the track onwards and away from the picnic site as far as a gap in the limestone ridge. Ignore any side tracks to your left.

❷ Do not go through the gap, but turn right and begin to climb steeply up the scrub-covered hillside, following a forestry track below the crest of the ridge.

❸ Continue ahead, still uphill when the forestry track swings right. Follow a wide path towards a tiny plateau at the foot of Mont Ste. Victoire. The refuge is in a small depression, but is easily seen from the approaching path.

❹ Take the path on the right as you face the refuge, going downhill in and out of rugged juniper covered hummocks and rocky outcrops, as far as the road.

❺ Turn left at the road, following it over a bridge, the oddly named *Pont de l'Anchois* (Bridge of the Anchovies). Continue ahead at the road junction then bear right and uphill into the attractive little hamlet of mostly modern houses, Le Bouquet.

❻ At the wide, open junction at the top of the narrow lane, and marked by a wisteria bush, go half left uphill, then right on to a rough track in front of an old house. Go past the 'No Entry' sign and follow a fairly level track across the scrub-covered hillside. As you pass by a water tank, begin to go downhill and swing to the left with the direction of the track.

❼ Turn right at the track junction and go steeply downhill and out of the rough forest. Go through a gate and turn left when joining another track, opposite an olive grove. Follow the now improving surface, past a wayside shrine and into the village of Beaurecueil.

❽ Turn right and follow the road through the village. At the far end go to the left with it for about forty metres, then right at a T-junction to follow the road past the château. Ignore side turnings and walk on past vineyards, olive groves, orchards and open meadows.

❾ Go to the right at the fork, then right again when joining the D17, the Route Cézanne. Continue for about 450 metres (quarter of a mile), over a bridge and turn left to follow the roadway signposted to the *Domaine Roques Hautes,* into the car park and picnic site.

Points of interest

Ⓐ Viewpoint overlooking the *Crête du Marbre,* the Marble Ridge. The particularly hard limestone of the nearby rocks makes an attractive marble when polished, prized since Roman times. Scrub oak and Corsican pines thrive on the arid slopes of the surrounding hills.

Ⓑ Viewpoint. Binoculars will be useful to pick out the tiny figures of rock climbers as they inch their way up the sheer south-facing walls of Mont Ste. Victoire.

Ⓒ Refuge Cézanne is typical of mountain huts found throughout the higher alpine regions. Simple but good food and accommodation is on offer. Every hut is built to a different style depending on its situation, but all have the same atmosphere of friendly camaraderie.

The site is a curious botanical mixture. Alpine flowers such as gentians and saxifrages blend with Mediterranean flora like the exquisite white St. Bernard's lily as well as aromatic rosemary and wild lavender bushes.

Ⓓ Viewpoint. It is necessary to walk so far away from the base of the mountain to appreciate the dramatic shape of Mont Ste. Victoire. Despite its comparative lack of height, it is only 945m (3,100ft) high, but from this angle the mountain looks positively alpine.

Walk 26
LACS BIMONT
& ZOLA

8 km (5 miles)   Moderate
104 metres (341ft) ascent and descent

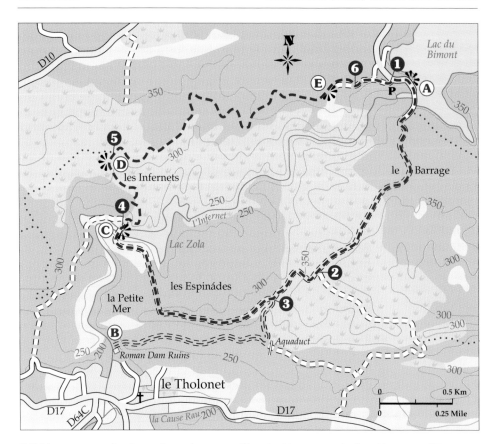

Reliable water supplies have always been a problem in this comparatively arid corner of Provençe. The River Infernet drains a high plateau to the east of Aix, but can only be relied upon to flow during winter or early spring. This precious flow has been collected since Roman times by damming a gorge a short distance from Aix in the foothills of Mont Ste. Victoire. Only a few stones are left of the Roman dam, but upstream, the first reservoir, dedicated to the writer Émile Zola, is now overtopped by a massive concrete wall holding back the waters of Lac du Bimont.

The French Impressionist painter Paul Cézanne walked the surrounding hills and forests. A short distance further east is a château on the spur of a hill overlooking Vauvenargues. It was here the modernist artist Pablo Picasso, banned from his native Spain by Franco's regime, spent his last years. It is also where he is buried, but the parkland site is private.

The scenery enjoyed on this walk is delightful and is what gave Cézanne much of his inspiration. Starting at Lac du Bimont, the walk follows reasonably level forest tracks before descending steadily towards Lac Zola. Here a short but steep climb leads to easier ground high above the narrow gorge. As the path climbing the 79 metres (259 feet) from Lac Zola can be slippery, strong footwear is recommended for this walk.

There are no restaurants or cafés on this walk, the nearest being in Aix. Alternatively, a picnic should be carried, or left in the car to await your return.

It is strongly recommended that a drink should be carried on this walk.

How to get there: Take the D10 Vauvenargues road east out of Aix for five kilometres (three miles). Turn right on the side road leading down to Lac du Bimont. Park near the dam. NB The direction of the reservoir is not well signposted. Look out for the turning on the right after passing open fields on your left beyond the village of les Savoyards.

Route description

❶ Walk past the road barrier and down to the dam wall. Cross to the other side and follow a sandy track, at first steeply, then over a series of low pine-covered rocky hillocks. Ignore minor side turnings, especially the one to the left signposted to Mont Ste. Victoire and the Croix de Provençe.

❷ Take the right fork at the track junction and begin to go downhill, gently at first, then more steeply into a side valley.

❸ Take the right fork again at a track junction in the valley bottom. Climb to the top of a south-facing limestone escarp-ment. Walk along the top of the crags, then downhill along a narrowing ridge, to make the last short but steep descent to the dam wall.

❹ Cross over to the opposite side of the gorge by following the access track away from the dam. Bear right, then left around a sharp left-hand bend. Go half way round the bend, and turn right on to a steeply rising path. Follow the path up the steep, scrub-covered rocky hillside to the lip of the dramatically out-cropping limestone gorge.

❺ Go through a line of rocks and turn right. Follow a winding path along the escarpment edge, high above the narrow gorge.

❻ Join the access track from the abandoned quarry and follow it back to the car park.

Points of interest

Ⓐ Viewpoint. Look over from the viewing platform towards the foot of the dam and the powerful outflow of water released from Lac du Bimont. The reservoir fills the upper part of a deep limestone gorge. Across the headwaters of the lake, and topped by the Croix de Provençe, rises the huge bulk of Mont Ste. Victoire. The present 18m (60ft) high cross continues a tradition begun in the sixteenth century. The priory of Ste. Victoire is only a short distance from the summit, and although its foundations go back to a simple hermit's cell dating from the fifth century, the present building is basically a restored seventeenth-century structure.

Ⓑ An optional diversion at this point leads to the remains of a Roman dam, the first to divert the waters of the Infernet. To reach the dam, walk down the track fol-lowing the narrow side valley until it reaches an aqueduct. Turn right here to climb the rocky, scrub-covered hillside to the Roman remains. Retrace your steps uphill to route pointer ❸ in order to continue the walk.

Ⓒ Viewpoint. Lac Zola fills the depths of the steep limestone gorge. Ravens and birds of prey nest on its rocky ledges, screened by the stunted growth of naturally bonsai'd Corsican pines and dwarf oak and juniper.

Ⓓ Viewpoint. Aix-en-Provençe, the capital of Provençe, spreads around its easily recognisable

ancient centre. Hot springs still flow from the Fontaine Chaude in the centre of the main boulevard, the Cours Mirabeau, as they did when the Romans founded their *Aquae Sextiae Saluviorum* here in 122BC. The water, mildly radio-active and containing a range of minerals, reaches the surface at a constant 36°C (97°F).

The Cours Mirabeau is the social heart of Aix. Seventeenth-century town mansions, their façades supported by nubile caryatids, line the Cours, sheltering behind solid doors and further protected by wrought-iron work. Smart shops line pedestrianised side streets, and to the north of the once-walled older part of the city is the cathedral.

Aix's town hall, the *Hôtel de Ville*, contains a library of over 300,000 ancient books and manuscripts, as well as the modern works of luminaries such as the Nobel Prize for Literature winner, the poet St. John Perse. Outside in the square is the *Flamboyant,* a clock tower which dates from 1520. Wooden statues represent the four seasons, each one visible for its four months, and below them are the modern statues of Day and Night. Topping them all is an astronomical clock made in 1661 and a Provençal bell-cage.

The Natural History Museum in the *Hôtel Boyer d'Eguilles* contains, amongst other exhibits, a collection of dinosaur's eggs, a selection of the thousands found in the rocks of Mont Ste. Victoire.

Walk 27
ST. CANNAT

8 km (5 miles)   Easy/Moderate

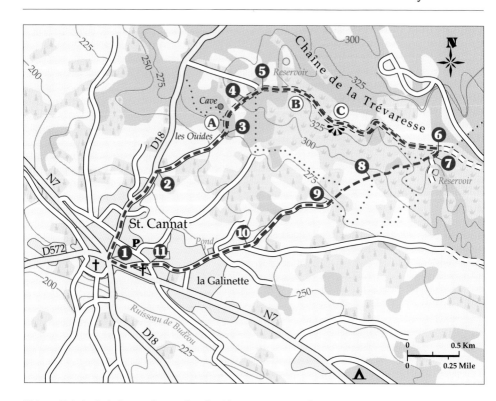

This walk is included as a pleasant break, either in its own right to explore the countryside around a small rural town, or simply to escape the pressures of driving along the all too frequently crowded main roads of southern Provençe. Even though the Autoroute du Soleil takes most of the traffic, the older roads such as the N7 between Aix and Cavaillon can still be tiresome, especially when the Mistral is blowing.

St. Cannat is a particularly traffic-troubled town. Despite its narrow streets, heavy lorries and holiday traffic must come this way when journeying from eastern and southern Provençe towards Cavaillon. The road to Arles and the Camargue leaves the N7 here, causing its own snarl-ups as traffic tries to turn against the main north-south flow. If the traffic is particularly heavy it is tempting and also wise to pull off the road.

Having left the main road, the backstreets of St. Cannat are blissfully quiet. The street pattern surrounding the church in the oldest part of the town hints at a once-fortified town. A quaintly pompous statue of Bailli de Saffren seems to look down with disapproval from its plinth at the road junction in the town centre. He was one of St. Cannat's worthy sons who was born in 1729 and died in Paris in 1788. He campaigned against the British in the struggle for supremacy in the West Indies.

The walk starts in the modern part of the town, in the Esplanade Général de Gaulle, then moves out of town on to the pine-clad Chaîne de la Trévaresse. The ridge, its south face carved by steeply indented dry valleys, is typical of the lines of marble hills marching purposefully towards the Mediterranean Sea. Most of the high ground in Provençe was created by conflicting land masses attempting to move together when the Alps and Pyrénées were built. Despite their lack of height, The Chaîne, like the other ridges in this part of south-western Provençe, barely manage to climb above the 400 metre level, but they always look mountainous.

Restaurants and bars line the backstreets of the old town and there is a good selection of shops. Children will love the Village des Automates just off the N7 in the direction of Aix. The 'village' is a collection of automated objects and rides set in woodland about three kilometres (two miles) from St. Cannat. There is also a small zoo of European and foreign birds and wild animals at the Château de la Barben. The château is a little to the north of the D572 Pélissanne and Salon-de-Provençe road, about eight kilometres (five miles) west of St. Cannat.

How to get there: St. Cannat is at the junction of the D572 Salon-de-Provençe road and the N7 Aix to Cavaillon road. Park away from the main road, to the north of the town centre, beside the tree-shaded Esplanade Général de Gaulle.

Route description

❶ Follow the side road, the D18 signposted to Rognes, for about 800 metres (875 yards) away from St. Cannat and as far as vineyards on the outskirts of the town.

❷ Turn right along a side lane called the Chemin des Ouides, past scattered properties, small vineyards and open fields and flowery meadows.

❸ Where the surfaced road ends, continue along a sandy track bearing left for a short distance. Take the furthest right fork where the track divides into three, and go uphill at a track junction. Climb through scrub woodland, then go past several vineyards and orchards.

❹ Ignoring side tracks into fields and vineyards to the left and right, follow the main track, bearing a little to your right and uphill into pine forest.

❺ Turn right on reaching the crest of the ridge and follow a wider, partly surfaced track, along the pine-clad Chaîne de la Trévaresse. Ignoring side tracks and driveways to isolated properties, follow the track a little to the right of the crest of the ridge for about two kilometres (1¼ miles).

❻ Turn right and go down the access track towards a small reservoir.

❼ Take the footpath continuing ahead where the track bears left towards the reservoir. Go forwards and downhill through woodland when a level path leaves to the right. Bear right, still downhill at the next junction.

❽ Take the right fork again, go between two ruined buildings, over a bridge and through vineyards. Ignore side turnings and continue downhill on the now easier gradient.

❾ Join a surfaced lane and follow it past scattered houses and farms, between vineyards, cultivated land and meadows.

❿ Bear right at the road junction and walk on over a staggered crossroads next to a small square pond, then on towards the outskirts of St. Cannat.

⓫ Go over the crossroads, past a church and turn right on reaching the main road. Follow it towards the town centre and take the first road on your right to reach the car park beside the Esplanade Général de Gaulle.

Points of interest

Ⓐ The next path to the left of route pointer ❸ leads a little way uphill to a small cave partly hidden by the rampant lush undergrowth. It is worth investigating, but only from the surface. Unless you are properly equipped and someone close by knows your exact plans, it is unwise to venture alone below ground.

Ⓑ Huge pine cones litter the track; fortunately they do not seem to drop on passing walkers.

Ⓒ Viewpoint. Gaps in the pine forest overlook a broad and fertile valley backed by the Chaîne d'Eguilles, the twin of the ridge you are standing on, the Chaîne de la Trévaresse. To the south-east is Aix-en-Provençe, and on a clear day you should be able to pick out Cézanne's beloved Mont Ste. Victoire on the far side of Aix. Salon-de-Provençe, to the west, is the centre of olive oil production in Provençe. Adam de Craponne, who built many of the irrigation canals carrying essential water throughout Provençe, was born here in 1519. The astrologer, Nostradamus, whose sixteenth-century predictions are still pondered over, once lived in Salon. A museum in the Château de l'Empéri traces the history of the French Army from the Middle Ages, through the Napoleonic era, to World War I.

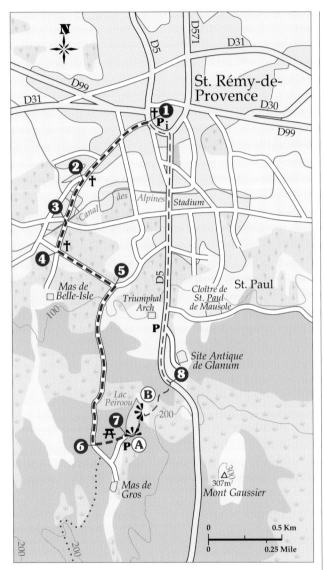

rock ledges are sometimes rather wide apart, the route is unsuitable for very small children. However, as Lac Peiroou, at the foot of the rock chimney, is easy to reach and is even accessible by car, a compromise could be made whereby the less able members of your party could return from the lake, meeting the 'climbing party' back at St. Rémy, or at some other pre-arranged place and time.

Option 'A', the Easy walk, returns from route pointer ❼, while the Strenuous Option 'B' continues, following the described walk.

Surrounded by orchards and market gardens, and backed by the startling white of the Alpilles hills, St-Rémy-de-Provence has retained its medieval feel, despite the traffic which splutters around its ancient heart. You can still find the house where the astrologer, Nostradamus, was born in 1503. Originally the physician to Charles IX, he was sacked for keeping his remedies secret, and turned to astrology, one suspects, in revenge. The handsome sixteenth-century town mansion which houses the Museé Alpilles Pierre de Brun, contains relics of Nostradamus, a man who has become something of a cult figure.

Another museum in the town centre is the Hôtel de Sade, once the home of relatives of the notorious marquis whose evil acts have given us the word 'sadism'. Here you will find items discovered on the site of *Glanum*, the Roman remains beyond the southern outskirts of St. Rémy (for

Strictly, this walk should be described as a short scramble through a rock chimney at the end of a pleasant woodland stroll. Later on in the walk, a road takes you past the magnificent remains of a Roman triumphal arch. Climbing the chimney is aided by the rungs of an iron ladder, but as those rungs and one or two adjacent

further details of this site, see Walk 29.

Bull-fighting is not to everyone's taste, especially the cruel Spanish version which is also practised in Provençe. However, there is another form of bull-fighting peculiar to Provençe, where the bull, though tormented, is not killed. Rosettes attached to the bull's horns and neck are snatched by highly agile participants who are then awarded monetary prizes. St. Rémy's arena is almost hidden in one of the backstreets off the D5 Maussanne road. Dates and times of the bull fights, *corridas*, both the Spanish and Provençal forms, are advertised locally.

Many of van Gogh's paintings deal with subjects around this lovely old town. Flowery meadows, gardens filled with irises, strangely shaped rock formations and pine trees similar to those he painted, will be seen on the walk.

There are no refreshments available on this walk, but St. Rémy is well stocked with shops, crêperies, cafés and restaurants.

How to get there: St-Rémy-de-Provençe sits at the junction of the D571 (Châteaurenard), D99 (Cavaillon-Tarascon) and D5 (Maussanne) roads. While parking is available in the town centre, it is usually fully occupied from early morning. There is a larger alternative car park next to the Tourist Information Office beside the Maussanne road, a little to the south of the town centre.

Route description

❶ With your back to the church steps in St. Rémy, turn half left and cross over to the town centre car park next to the war memorial. Cross the car park diagonally left, then bear right to follow the side road. Follow the road out of St. Rémy for about 500 metres (a little over a quarter of a mile).

❷ Bear left at a road fork marked by a wayside calvary on your left, and walk on past small vineyards, orchards and olive groves. Go over a narrow irrigation canal and past a tennis court on your right.

❸ Turn sharp left to cross another irrigation canal, then right at the road junction beyond the bridge. Begin to walk steadily uphill.

❹ Turn left at the crossroads marked by a wayside shrine. Walk on past scattered properties and between orchards and olive groves.

❺ Turn right at the T-junction and follow the lane signposted to *le Barrage*, uphill through a narrow cutting and head towards the pine-clad rocky hillside.

❻ Where the lane begins to level out, and within sight of the crag embowered reservoir, turn left, downhill on a path winding between mature pines. (If you are not certain which path to take, remember to look out for the reservoir before turning. Alternatively, continue to follow the lane, as it will arrive at the same destination.) The easier Option 'A' ends at Lac Peiroou and, after exploring the shoreline, retraces the route back to St. Rémy.

❼ Option 'B'. From the car park and picnic site, follow the shoreline to the left. There are a number of confusing paths created by fishermen, but to keep to the correct one, follow white/red or occasional yellow waymarks.

The path winds its way uphill, over outcropping rocks, towards the seemingly impossible foot of a huge overhanging limestone crag. On reaching this, turn right with the path, steeply uphill, on a well engineered route towards a massive hole. Climb to the left, then right into the 'chimney' and scramble, with care, up the rock steps and iron rungs. Even though the hole penetrates the crag from one side to the other, there should be plenty of light to see the way.

At the top of the climb, bear left then right with the path, then generally left through the trees to reach a stone ramp leading down to the road. The path joins the road below a blind corner, so take care not to step out into the path of oncoming vehicles.

❽ Keep on the lookout for cars and walk on the left-hand side of the road all the way into St. Rémy. Pass the entrance to *Glanum* on the right, and also the triumphal arch, to the left.

Points of interest

Ⓐ It is hard to believe that the Barrage des Peiroou is a man-made lake. In its tree-lined setting at the foot of a limestone amphitheatre, the reservoir looks quite natural. The tiny dam wall is well hidden in the narrow gap between two rounded crags. Providing St. Rémy with drinking water, the reservoir is popular with local anglers. Cragsmen test their skills on the massive limestone walls overtopping the reservoir to your right.

Ⓑ Viewpoint. The walls of the chimney frame an attractive view of the lake and pine forest. Well placed iron rungs and maintained rock steps make the ascent relatively easy.

Walk 29
ROCHER DES DEUX TROUS 7 km (4¼ miles) Moderate/Strenuous

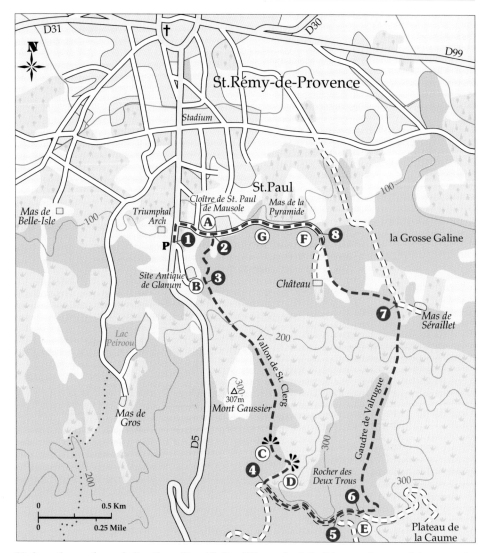

High on the southern skyline the rolling Alpilles hills overlook St. Rémy, and one rock in particular stands out. Surrounded by aromatic shrubs and dwarf Corsican pines, the twin holes which gave *le Rocher des Deux Trous* its name are clearly visible even from the town.

Vincent van Gogh was fascinated by the contorted shapes of the Alpilles ridge and it features as the background of many of his paintings. The two holes cut through *le Rocher des Deux Trous* show clearly on van Gogh's *les oliviers* (the olive trees), which was painted from a viewpoint a little way above the cloister of St. Paul de Mausole. This was where van Gogh was cared for after one of his violent spells of insanity; the tranquil scene is unchanged after more than a century.

The walk starts close by the cloister and almost immediately skirts the excavated remains of the exquisite little Roman town of *Glanum*. Flower-filled meadows soon give way to tracks baked hard by the summer sun; box grows at shoulder level in the dense woodland, where the dappled shade of Corsican pines and the occasional Atlas cedar come as a welcome relief during the stiff climb. The ridge-top and its strangely worn rocks is covered by aromatics. The scent of crushed pine underfoot competes with the heady aroma of lavender and the subtle smell of rosemary. Lizards bask in the warmth, and countless butterflies seek the nectar from vivid blue mountain cornflower or lavender sprays. The return leg of the walk follows the sun-trapped gorge of the *Gaudre de Valrugue* down to a hideaway farm, and from there a woodland track leads out towards the orchards and meadows of St. Rémy.

Fire is an ever-present hazard in Provençal forests. Tinder dry in summer, a smouldering cigarette end could start a fire that would wipe out hundreds of hectares of ancient woodland in a terrifyingly short time. Groups of more than six persons are not allowed in the highly sensitive zone covered by this walk.

There are no places to stop for refreshments on this walk, but St. Rémy is close by. A carried drink is recommended.

How to get there: Drive south from St. Rémy for a kilometre (just over half a mile) and park at the roadside car park next to the *Glanum* site. If staying in St. Rémy it will probably be easier to leave the car there and walk the short way up the road.

Route description

❶ From the *Glanum* car park walk along the road in the direction of St. Rémy, past the triumphal arch and mausoleum. Turn right to follow the lane which skirts the cloister of St. Paul de Mausole for about 220 metres (240yds).

❷ Turn right on to a side lane signposted *les Deux Trous,* then left at the second turning. Follow a woodland path, at first alongside the perimeter fence enclosing *Glanum,* then begin to climb.

❸ Beyond the limits of the Roman town, go slightly downhill, then increasingly steeply uphill along the dry valley bottom. Bear left with the valley to clear a natural break in a line of outcropping crags. Swing right even more steeply with the path to reach a small col and then onwards to the ridge.

❹ Go to the left on reaching the narrow ridge-top, following a forestry track.

❺ Continue ahead at a track crossing, along a slightly wider part of the ridge.

❻ Turn left on to the side track going steeply downhill into the upper part of the dry *Gaudre de Valrugue*. Swing left again as the path loses height, then slightly right on reaching the valley bottom. The descent is easier for the next 750 metres (820yds), before dropping rather more steeply through the gap in a narrow rocky outcrop in order to reach an olive grove bordering a small farm.

❼ Look for yellow waymarks on trees to the left of the signposted turning to the Mas de Séraillet. Turn left and follow the waymarks. The woodland path is indistinct at first as it climbs a slight rise, but improves where it descends to the right of a small secluded château. Ignore access drives leading to the château.

❽ Go to the right of the château estate gates and into a shaded hollow, then bear left on a gradually improving level track. Follow what becomes a surfaced lane all the way back, past the cloister and onward to the main road. *Glanum* car park is to your left.

Points of interest

Ⓐ Visit the cloister of St. Paul de Mausole where van Gogh became a voluntary patient for a year in 1889, soon after he cut off his ear. It is possible that part of his madness was caused by drinking absinthe, the much stronger and now illegal forerunner of pastis. Tranquil gardens fill the central quadrangle.

Ⓑ *Glanum* was a high-class retreat for the privileged Roman few. Much of the site has been carefully excavated, leading to the discovery that it had been inhabited since Neolithic times. The triumphal arch at the start of the walk is part of the yet unexcavated ruins and was cut by the *Via Domitia* which linked *Glanum* to the important port of *Arelate* on the site of the modern city of Arles. Reliefs commemorate Julius Caesar's victories over the Gauls and Greeks at *Massalia* (Marseille) in 49BC. The mausoleum next to the arch is to the memory of Caesar's two adopted sons.

Ⓒ Viewpoint looking back towards St. Rémy and the la Montagnette ridge, the sister ridge of les Alpilles.

Ⓓ Viewpoint. The two holes in *le Rocher les Deux Trous* was made by the action of wind and rain over countless centuries.

Ⓔ Spend time looking for lizards, butterflies and unusual plants.

Ⓕ The quarry behind the old house on the left provided building stone for nearby *Glanum*.

Ⓖ Le Mas de la Pyramide. The farm, which is open to visitors, is set in the middle of a Roman quarry, part of which was a troglodyte dwelling. A massive rock set amongst lavender fields gives the place its name.

Walk 30
LES BAUX

6 km (3¾ miles) Easy/Moderate

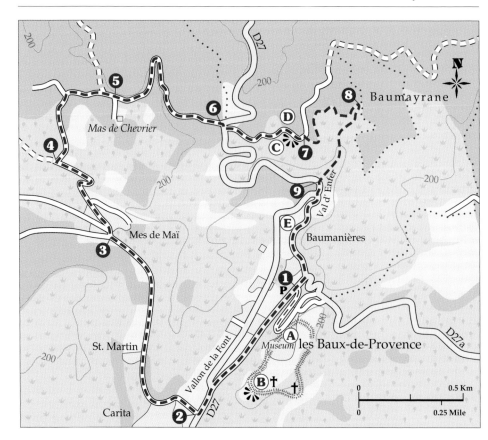

Everyone who comes to Provençe should make at least one visit to les Baux. The citadel town sits on top of a bare limestone ridge overlooking the Rhône estuary. Houses dating from the fourteenth century are literally carved from the living rock, huddling close to the now-ruined hilltop castle.

Les Baux has been inhabited since prehistoric people made themselves a fortified *oppidum* on the furthest tip of the flat-topped ridge. Controlled by the Lords of Les Baux from the eleventh to the fifteenth century, the town became famous for its 'Courts of Love'. Turning Protestant in the seventeenth century brought the wrath of Louis XIII on the town, and, with its ramparts destroyed, the place went into decay.

The walk is intended to be part of a visit to Les Baux. From the town, quiet lanes and forestry tracks climb the Châine des Alpilles, where ever-changing views of the ridge-top citadel and the hazy fertile plain unfold.

Les Baux has everything to offer in the way of food, from simple crêperies to the internationally renowned les Baumanières Restaurant, where the bill is likely to be as spectacular as the scenery. H.M. Queen Elizabeth II and Prince Philip, the Duke of Edinburgh, were entertained there on an informal visit to Les Baux.

How to get there: Les Baux stands above the D27 St. Rémy to Maussane road, about 2.5 kilometres (1¹/2 miles) north-west of Maussane, where the D17 is joined by the D5. Park at the roadside below and to the west of Les Baux.

Route description

1 Climb up to Les Baux by way of the narrow lane angling up towards the ancient ramparts. Retrace your steps to the main road and turn left, downhill.

2 Take the second road on the right and cross the narrow fertile Vallon de la Font, then begin to climb, swinging right around the foot of the steeply protruding scrub-covered limestone spur. Follow the embanked road past a number of properties and small orchards and olive groves.

3 Turn right at the fork and immediately right again, climbing uphill along the narrow lane through the hillside village of Mes de Maï. Go through the gap in a line of crags overlooking the village. Swing round a tight bend, and, ignoring side tracks, go down to a fairly flat area filled with olive groves and orchards.

4 Turn right at the T-junction and begin to climb, past a small farmhouse surrounded by vineyards, easily at first, then more steeply into scrub woodland. Ignore two side turnings and follow the woodland road as it swings to the right towards the steepest pine-clad upper slopes.

5 Go over the crossroads, continuing to climb. Move towards then round the head of a dry valley. Strategically placed bench seats here offer fine views and take much of the effort out of the climb.

6 At the col, cross the main road, the D27, by bearing right and almost immediately left to follow a forest road climbing towards the ridge-top.

7 Go to the right, opposite the side turning to the 'Table d'Orientation', and go steeply downhill, along a forest track swinging left and into a steep-sided dry valley.

8 Turn sharp right at the cross tracks, downhill through the forest and into *Val d'Enfer*, the 'Valley of Hell'.

9 Turn left when you join the road, following it downhill past a side road on your right and past various commercial attractions, heading steadily towards Les Baux. Turn right at the road junction below the northern end of the citadel to reach route pointer **1** and the start of the walk.

Points of interest

A Ancient alleyways lined with attractive cottages lead upwards towards the Museum of Les Baux, where exhibits explain the once romantic, but often bloody history of Les Baux. Beyond are the remains of the once proud citadel. Walk towards the lip where the Orientation Table points out the towns and hills surrounding the Rhône delta. Taking care not to go too close to the edge, follow the rim past reconstructed siege weapons, to reach the high ramparts before exploring the rest of the site and the village streets.

A leaflet, in English, describes all the features and the story of Les Baux. Ask for one on entering the museum.

B Viewpoint. Looking from the southern ramparts across an olive grove-filled dry plain and towards the distant glint of the Mediterranean Sea.

C The natural 'temple of the winds' has been created by the action of wind and rain over countless millenia. Children love to climb its contorted sides, but make sure they do not become over-ambitious on its more exposed parts.

D Viewpoint. A *Table d'Orientation* uphill and to the left of the forestry track looks out across the olive groves and cherry orchards below Les Baux and out towards the hazy limits of the Bouches de Rhône. On days when the Mistral blows down the Rhône valley the view is clearer.

E *Val d'Enfer*. The 'Valley of Hell' is cut through a special form of aluminium limestone, Bauxite, which takes its name from Les Baux. Quarried since Roman times, many of the caverns created by the search for this valuable material are used as wine caves. Offers to sample the vintages *(dégustations)* abound and it will be the most self-willed walker who can resist. The *Cathedral d'Images* is a unique experience. Forty projectors present an audiovisual display of images, creating ancient temples and futuristic pictures on the massive walls.

BARTHOLOMEW WALK GUIDES

Bartholomew publishes an extensive range of Walk Guides
covering some of the best walking country in Britain and France.

Titles in the series include:

Walking in Brittany
Walking in the Dordogne
Walking in the Loire Valley

Walk the Cornish Coastal Path
Walk the Cotswolds
Walk the Dales
Walk Dorset & Thomas Hardy's Wessex
Walk Kent
Walk the Lakes
More Walks in the Lakes
Walk Loch Lomond & the Trossachs
Walk Loch Ness & the Spey Valley
Walk the New Forest
Walk the North York Moors
Walk Northumbria
Walk Oban, Mull & Lochaber
Walk the Peak District
Walk Perthshire
Walk Skye & Wester Ross
Walk Snowdonia & North Wales
Walk South Devon Coastal Path & Dartmoor

All titles are available from good bookshops,
or telephone HarperCollins Distribution Services
on 0141-772 3200.